# The Remarkable Women
of Ancient Egypt

# The Remarkable Women of Ancient Egypt

by Barbara S. Lesko

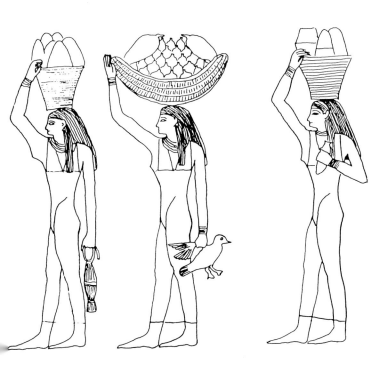

**B. C. Scribe Publications**
**P. O. Box 2453**
**Providence, RI 02906**

**Third Edition (revised and enlarged)**
**Copyright © 1996 by Barbara S. Lesko**
**Printed in the United States of America**

*Title Page*

Line of female farmworkers in the
tomb of Ti, Fifth Dynasty, Sakkara.
    Line drawing by L. H. Lesko

ISBN 0-930548-13-2

# *Preface*

This third edition follows the recent surge in research and writing on ancient Egyptian women which, I like to think, was spurred by our 1987 Conference on Women in Ancient Egypt and Western Asia held at Brown University and funded by its Department of Egyptology, the National Endowment for the Humanities, and the Mellon Foundation. Because of its size, readable style, and illustrations, this modest book, privately printed, has enjoyed a spectacular success, selling out each edition. Because of constant inquiries about its availability, I decided to bring out still another expanded version, benefiting from current research and inspired by the realization that some other authors tend not to see the forest for the trees, or, to put it another way, to see the glass half empty, whereas I admit to seeing it half full--having always been struck by the legal advantages ancient Egyptian women possessed throughout history and by the high visibility they maintained for many centuries on the monuments. Having read widely through anthropological and historical studies of women in other cultures, I understand that all civilized societies have been male dominated, but there are still enough differences between Egyptian women and their ancient and more modern sisters to be worth writing about.

Doubtless some statements in this book will be altered in years to come due to new discoveries, and I have included a greatly expanded bibliography to encourage and aid the students attracted to piecing together women's earliest story.

Grateful thanks go to my friend of many years Dr. Gamal Mokhtar, past President of the Organization of Egyptian Antiquities and to his present successor Professor Abd el-Halim Nur el-Din and to Dr. Aly Hassan, former Director, and Dr. Mohammed Saleh, present Director, of Cairo's Egyptian Musem of Antiquities for permission to photograph and use as illustrations monuments in Egypt. Thanks also must go to Dr. Christine Lilyquist and Dr. Dorothea Arnold of New York's Metropolitan Museum of Art, Mme. Ch. Desroches Noblecourt of the Louvre, Dr. T. G. H. James of the British Museum, Dr. Jürgen Settgast of the Egyptian Museum in Berlin (then Charlottenburg), Dr. Wm. K. Simpson and Dr. Rita Freed of the Museum of Fine Arts in Boston, Professor Donald B. Redford, University of Toronto, to the staff of the Egypt Exploration Society, London, and the Phoebe Apperson Hearst Museum of the University of California, Berkeley, for permission to publish photos or facsimiles of objects from their collections. It is a pleasure to give credit to Susan Weeks for line drawings and to my husband Leonard H. Lesko, Wilbour Chair Professor of Egyptology at Brown University, for his expert editorial and photographic contributions.

I am happy once again to be able to dedicate this little book to Leonard and to my parents for their valued and constant encouragement over the years.

Barbara Switalski Lesko
June, 1996

# *Introduction*

**Four thousand years ago** the women of Egypt enjoyed more legal rights and privileges than women have in many nations of today's world. Equal pay for equal work is a cry heard now but was practiced thousands of years ago in Egypt. Whether as an employee of the State, a vendor in the marketplace, the manager of a household, or as an active participant among the clergy in the religious hierarchies, the ancient Egyptian woman held a vital place in her society that amazed and bewildered foreign contemporaries who observed her.

The position of women (just like that of men) underwent changes during ancient Egypt's three-thousand year history, but one feature--the principle of legal equality--was basic to the Egyptian culture in antiquity. The patriarchal family structure, so pronounced among many other ancient peoples, is found only in a diluted form among the Egyptians. Men dominated in public life, but women were not restricted to the domicile and were regarded by the State as mature adults, responsible for their own actions. Both sexes were regarded as full legal personalities. In private life women were far freer and more independent than their sisters in most other ancient societies appear to have been.

Women's social status, activities, legal and economic rights during pharaonic times are today traceable through the art on private monuments and the written documentation that has survived. The Egyptian's literature--wisdom texts, short stories, and love songs--is revealing of customs and attitudes. These and the art, however, are the work of men and thus reflect their interests and biases. The most helpful documents are rather the private letters, wills, property deeds, tax rolls and marriage and adoption records that have survived. Some of these were inscribed on durable flakes of limestone and broken pieces of pottery (ostraca), but the most important were usually written on more expensive (and also much more fragile and destructible) sheets or rolls of papyrus paper.

Because papyri easily deteriorated over the course of centuries, far more such evidence has survived from antiquity's later chapters than from her earlier ones. This has led to a somewhat lop-sided reconstruction of past social history with more known, for instance, about marriage and property settlements of Egypt's Persian and Ptolemaic periods (last five centuries B.C.) than about such arrangements in the age of the pyramid builders (Old Kingdom, 2700-2190 B.C.) or even the Empire Period (New Kingdom, 1552-1069 B.C.).

Menkaure of the Fourth Dynasty and his queen Khamerernebty II. Photo by L. H. Lesko. Permission to reproduce courtesy of the Boston Museum of Fine Arts.

Even so, some of the information on tax rolls or in the last wills and testaments dating from the Empire Period corresponds remarkably well with what is known of women's legal status and the inheritance practices of five hundred to a thousand years later. This leads us to believe that the laws and customs of the later Persian and Ptolemaic periods may well have been similar in essential features to those practiced at the height of pharaonic rule. This study will limit itself to that pharaonic period and proceeds in full realization that phenomenological studies can err through generalizations, but space does not permit us here to deal systematically with every period of Egyptian history. Indeed, the status of women did seem to wax and wane, by our standards, with the fortunes of the country, and some eras saw women seemingly more involved in the public life than they were at other times. Gender was an important determining factor influencing life's possibilities, but also social status controlled the destinies of most people.

Pharaoh Thutmose III being suckled by the goddess Hathor in her form of a sycamore tree. From the King's tomb, Thebes.

Photo by L. H. Lesko

# DIVINE WOMEN / ROYAL WOMEN

The names Hatshepsut and Nefertiti are widely recognized as ancient Egyptian queens, and surely if we had no other names from Egypt's long history we would still be able to call up, from just these two, reliable images of alluring and strong women, remarkable for their daring ambition and the leadership they exerted. Fortunately, we can write volumes about ancient Egyptian history and culture and have much information on the women, both royal and non royal. The written sources extend over a history 3000 years long which has left us a plethora of names and images of Egypt's rulers and ruled. Among these are other able queens and female pharaohs. The extensive artistic and written records have allowed us to flesh out Hatshepsut and Nefertiti and add to them the remarkable careers of their female relatives and images of many of their female subjects.

Because of the preservation of a huge corpus of source material, we can truly say that women's history, her longest continuous story, begins here in Africa in the verdant valley of the Nile. Here the earliest testaments to goddesses, queens, priestesses and more ordinary women have been found by archaeologists.

*First, however, we must look at the female leaders who were present even before there was a queen of Egypt.*

From the time before there was a state--before the union between the two kingdoms of Upper and Lower Egypt which occurred around 3100 B.C.-- that is, from the prehistoric/predynastic age, survive some large graves belonging to women, supplied with the weapons associated with men, supplied too with small images of males, as if companions for the deceased important female (Baumgartel, 1955, 35). It is tempting to see in such graves and in their ceramic pottery's decoration (depicting large females accompanied by smaller female and male figures) a dominating leadership role, whether political or religious, for women in prehistoric Egypt. This is a factor well known from African societies of later periods, and Egypt was an African culture (Leacock, 1981, 20). Therefore, we should not expect Egypt's most ancient periods to reflect patterns of culture in the ancient Near Eastern or Aegean worlds. Before studying the queens of Egypt, let us acknowledge the goddesses they served.

# Goddesses

The prehistoric Egyptians worshipped goddesses, although not exclusively as symbols later associated with certain male divinities also appear and the Egyptians' first testaments of faith definitely involved animal clan divinities as well--cows, bulls and sheep were represented among the numerous figurines of animals as were the more threatening snakes and hippos. The carefully wrapped bodies of some animals were buried among those of humans in the earliest cemeteries. Rough pottery figurines of females are also found with the earliest burials discovered, dating from about 5000 B.C. Archaeologists think these had a religious significance but do not agree on what it was. One such figurine in particular might be taken as a representation of a goddess of fertility as its back is engraved with a plant motif (Adams, 1992, 13).

A human-formed goddess of fertility may well have taken shape in the minds of women at the dawn of the agricultural revolution and the domestication of animals--both of which could easily be the legacies of early womankind. Also from this prehistoric age bovine images are found on vases and small stone amulets. Evidence from elsewhere in Africa suggests that, when and where the female principle was venerated, it often assumed aspects of the cow. Indeed the cow still receives veneration today in herding societies. With the absence of texts from Egypt's prehistoric period we cannot understand all the nuances of the early goddesses' meaning for their people, but in the art and literature of Egypt's historic period the images of cow goddesses are prominent and they have many important roles to play.

Towards the end of Egypt's long prehistoric period, buff pottery with its red line paintings give the best insights into the culture of that time. Several deities known from later times are suggested by the totems portrayed in these paintings. Divine symbols include the crossed arrows of the goddess Neit and the harpoon-like spear or phallic symbol of the fertility god Min, and the falcon of Horus, a later sky god. The earliest clear representations of a cow goddess are found on slate palettes. One of these from the Gerzean Period bears a relief of a cow's head (facing forward) and five stars just above the tips of the horns. (Adams, 1988, 48). The curved horns remind one of the lunar crescent, and the celestial aspect is certainly emphasized by the presence of stars in this rendition.

## Bat

In about 3100 B.C., when the Upper Egyptians assumed control over the entire country, they commemorated their victory over the Delta on another commemorative palette, placing the cow goddess of Upper Egypt at the top of both sides of that votive object (the Narmer palette). The forward facing cow with the in-turned horns is later identified with the goddess Bat, but there were numerous goddesses linked to cow images.

## Nut

Even Nut (pronounced *noot*) the sky goddess was often portrayed as a cow, her four legs being the four supports of the heavenly canopy: the cow's star-studded belly. However Nut appears more frequently as a totally human female, nude and stretched out with toes on the eastern horizon and fingertips on the western. Because the worthy dead were expected to reach the heavens and unite with the stars which made up the body of this goddess, Nut is often portrayed inside coffins as the heavenly mother who will embrace the deceased.

Nut was regarded as Mother of the Gods but she was part of the original family, the daughter of the first couple Shu and Tefnut, air and moisture. According to one very early cosmological myth, the sky-goddess Nut and her brother the earth god Geb produced from their union the fertile mud of the Nile valley, Osiris, god of vegetation, and his brother, Seth, the barren desert. With their sisters, Isis and Nepthys, as consorts, these two brothers struggled for earthly rule.

## Isis

Once, perhaps long before recorded history, Osiris may have been an actual ruler, a good king who had been murdered and mutilated by his jealous brother. Osiris met a cruel fate, but, according to the myth, his sister-wife Isis roamed the earth collecting the dispersed pieces of her husband's body to reunite them and bring her spouse back to life long enough to conceive his heir. Isis hence forth would be famed for her magical powers. The son she subsequently bore was Horus, who would avenge his father and be the divine king of Egypt forever more. The earthly king on the Isis-throne (her name meant throne) was officially known as the living-Horus king--who was thought of, mythologically, as the grandson of Nut and son of Isis and Osiris. Osiris became king of the dead and, because of her ability to reconstitute and revive her husband, Isis and her loyal sister Nephthys were always to be a part of Egyptian funerals, mourning and protecting the deceased and helping Egypt's deserving dead to achieve immortal life. Because she promised ever-lasting life, Isis, of course, became a very popular deity. As time went on, her cult merged with or absorbed that of other Egyptian goddesses, and she became a universal goddess as her fame spread around the ancient world. Temples to Isis are found on three continents and as far north as Britain. Her cult continued in Egypt until the Fifth Century A. D.

## Hathor

Looked at later by other ancient theologians in a more abstract and intellectual manner, the divine kingship had a somewhat different origin. For them, the sun-god Re was the all encompassing supreme god who existed in the beginning and who created everything else. In the Re theology, the Horus king was the son of Re by his consort Hathor.

Hathor, which means "House of Horus," was herself the personification of the entire Ennead, i.e. Horus's genealogy--the five chthonic deities in addition to the brother-sister pair that actually bore Horus (Osiris and Isis) and their sibling rivals Seth and Nephthys (L.H. Lesko, 1991, 88-93). Re, Ptah (patron god of the capital city of Memphis), and Hathor were the three most important gods in the dynamic Old Kingdom period, which saw the building of the great pyramids. Certainly the queen of Egypt was seen as the manifestation of the goddess Hathor and also served as her high priestess. Hathor had many roles, she was the eye of the sun personifying its destructive power, but she was also the promoter of sex and fertility and, connected to this, the divine patroness of music and dance. As death was seen as an opportunity to be born anew in a better life, Hathor was also a participant in the funerary religion as the welcomer of the worthy dead at the gate to the Beyond. Eventually Hathor absorbed earlier cow goddesses and became frequently portrayed as a cow and divine nurse who suckles the royal heir. Even when she retains her human face, as on the capitals in her chapel at Deir el Bahri or her great temple at Dendera, the goddess's ears are those of a cow.

Illustration of the "Second Hour" from the Book of Amduat in the tomb of King Ramses IX. Isis and Nephthys as serpents guard the prow of the night bark of the sun-god shown as the ram headed Amon-Re in the kiosk preceded by the Lady of the Bark in the form of Hathor followed by the falcon headed Horus.

Photo by L. H. Lesko

### The Two Ladies

From an earlier prehistoric time, when the Two Lands of Upper and Lower Egypt were still separate entities, a goddess was preeminent in each. She protected the kingdom, and was regarded as ancestress of its ruling family. The Delta, its extensive swamps a haven for snakes, paid homage to a sacred cobra **Wadjet.** She would guard the king from all enemies and, to this end, sat upon his brow ready to strike any that threatened. In the south, where the barren cliffs and deserts of Upper Egypt encroached upon the fertile strip of river valley, a sacred vulture named **Nekhbet** held sway. After political union of the Two Lands, the Two Ladies became the titular goddesses of the royal house. One can find the images of both cobra and vulture on the brow of the golden mask of Tutankhamun, for instance. Throughout pharaonic history, the king had five royal titles and He of the Two Ladies recalled these most primeval protectresses.

### Neit

As already mentioned, one of the earliest identifiable totems on the predynastic painted pots was the crossed arrows of the goddess Neit. This is the goddess whose cult was probably concentrated in the northern kingdom, Lower Egypt, and centered on the ancient city of Sais in the Delta. Neit is usually shown wearing the red crown of Lower Egypt so she probably rivaled Wadjet as the preeminent deity there. Her sign was always that of crossed arrows, but her power seems to have extended to the creation of all that is, for she was still credited with creation by herself (through utterance) as late as the Roman Period in a great temple at Esna in the south of Egypt, whose theological texts must reflect the long-held views of her followers (Clagett, 1989, 578-580). The first queens--who may have been daughters of the royal house of the northern kingdom (or Lower Egypt)-- honored Neit with their names: Herneit, Meritneit and Neithotep being examples.

Until the very end of ancient Egyptian history and its religion all these six goddesses--Neit, Nut, Isis, Hathor, Wadjet and Nekhbet--were honored as the great maternal ancestors of the divine king of Egypt. Certainly, the queen of Egypt, who was expected to bear the next ruler, was seen as the manifestation of the Goddess Hathor and also served both her and Neit as a high priestess.

## Queens

Royal women--mothers, wives and daughters of the king--were featured on the monuments frequently, while their sons and brothers seldom appear, unless they achieved the throne or were the acknowledged heirs apparent. Queens were often represented singly and larger than life. Otherwise they shared the monuments of their consorts and were shown on equal scale with the king, or, if the image of the king was alone cast large, the name, title and figure of his mother or chief wife was still not absent. Thus the important roles of such women in the kingdom were acknowledged, and what these were will be the focus of our discussion.

Female monarchs are found right at the dawn of Egypt's history, probably due to their gaining rulership as regents for under-age sons who later became kings (Callendar, 1992, 52). It is significant that in Egypt the guardianship of the young heir to the throne was deemed the prerogative of his mother (or some senior female relative by blood or marriage) and was not handed over to a male relative (such as his father's brother). The story of Isis and Horus is the mythological support for this political decision.

The first queens of the historic dynasties were obviously followers of Neit, as the names of several include reference to this goddess. Early in the First Dynasty Neithotep's name is associated with an elaborate tomb of twenty-one chambers near the ancient Upper Egyptian capital at Naqada. She was either the wife or mother of King Aha second ruler of the First Dynasty, but as her name appears written within the exclusively kingly serekh design, it is likely that Neithotep was a queen-regnant. Similarly, the mother of King Den, Meritneit, used the serekh for her name and also owned two large tombs, one in the north and one in the south, as did the male monarchs of this dynasty (Edwards, 1971, 18-25).

The ancient classical historian Manetho recorded the passing of a law in the Second Dynasty permitting women to rule as king, so it seems possible that females did at least occasionally occupy the throne during these formative centuries of Egyptian nationhood, although the law may indicate a temporary abatement proceeded it's formulation.

The enormous expenditure on the tombs for queens and their similarity to those of kings leads us to suspect that at least during the earliest dynasties daughters of ruling families in the north (Lower Egypt) helped legitimize the rule of the king over a united kingdom of two lands by marrying the ascendant leader from Upper Egypt.

While the first royal marriages were probably between the two royal houses of Egypt, north and south, after a few generations the throne was kept within the royal family by marriages between siblings, at least half brothers and sisters, if not full. All the known queens of the Second and Third Dynasty held the title "king's daughter" (Troy, 1986, 152). By the late Twelfth Dynasty, the chief wife of the King of Egypt would be known as the Mistress of the Two Lands (Troy, 1986, 158), but the accumulation of her numerous titles began in the Old Kingdom and increased in the Fourth Dynasty. Some queenly titles express her relationship to major deities or to the divine king: She who sees Horus and Seth; Mother of the King of Upper and Lower Egypt. Others express cultic power: Great One of the *hts*-scepter; Prophet of Thoth; Priestess of Hathor (Troy, 1986, 152-156).

For generations, until the Fifth Dynasty (circa 2500 B.C.), the highest offices in government were filled by members of the royal family to keep all power concentrated, and the queen of Egypt filled vital roles for the nation. Queen Hetepheres II, for instance, was a "controller of the affairs of the kilt-wearers," who have been interpreted as high ranking male officials in the government (Callender, 1992, 24). While princesses often were the recipients of fine tombs all their own, their tomb inscriptions voice their father's wishes for his daughter's long life, happy after life, and perpetual offerings to her spirit. Unlike a male recipient of such a kingly gesture, the princess does not voice her own thoughts in her tomb inscriptions (Lichtheim, 1973, 16).

One Fifth Dynasty list records the names of the mothers of some of the first kings of Egypt who reigned centuries before the inscription was carved in stone--surely good evidence of the prime importance of those royal mothers (Clagett, 1989, 70-82). Royal mothers and chief wives shared with the king many prerogatives, not least of which was attainment of eternal life with the gods. We have already seen that the king, and probably the queen, was viewed as divine. Indeed, the queen at least as early as the Sixth Dynasty adopted the vulture headdress which linked her with the venerable goddess Nekhbet. She also is, like the king and deities, shown holding the divine sign of life, the *ankh*. Such insignia give credence to the concept of divinity for the principal wife of the ruler (Robins, 1993, 23-25).

Upon, death both king and queen exclusively had the right to be buried in pyramid tombs, supplied with boats (buried outside) which they would use when they joined the sun god who traversed the heavens on his celestial bark. Or the king and queen might be pulled up to the sky by Nut to become one of the imperishable stars (Pyramid Text Spell 571). In the Old Kingdom only the kings and queens were buried with the magical/religious spells which, by the Sixth Dynasty, were engraved on the interiors of the pyramids of both kings and queens, but which had surely been written on papyrus scrolls previously. These spells leave no doubt that both kings and queens became divinities and joined the great gods, continuing their existence on the heavenly plane.

While history has preserved few details about the lives of the early kings and queens of Egypt, we do know that queens officiated as high priestesses at important cult centers like the temple of Thoth, Min, Hathor and Neit, as well as at the funerary temples of the preceding kings--probably her own male relatives--at what was then probably the largest temple in the land (Fischer, 1982, 1101-2). Art in the tombs of royal females show them carried in sedan chairs by groups of female bearers and having male secretaries (Dunham, 1974, 16, pl. VIII; Malek, 1986, 50). Large estates and workshops were always associated with the queen's palaces and their tombs (as probably their homes) were outfitted with gold embossed furnishings (Killen, 1980, 28, 59; Malek, 1986, 63).

It is possible that as many as three women ruled over the nation for a time during the Old Kingdom. One was Queen Khentkawes whose great tomb, which has sometimes been called "the fourth pyramid of Giza," gives us her titles (Verner, 1980). These translate as Mother of the Two Kings of Upper and Lower Egypt, and she is believed to have been the dynastic link between the Fourth and Fifth Dynasty and possibly to have acted as regent for a time. Otherwise it is difficult to understand why she would have had such an imposing tomb built so independently, out in front of the three kings' pyramids of the earlier Fourth Dynasty. Another woman who was regent for her son was the Queen Ankhenesmerire II, a common-born wife of Pepi I, whose first queen disappointed him by committing some crime that was discovered and brought about her downfall (Grimal, 1992, 83). Actually Ankhenesmerire and her sister were both married by the king, following this scandal. By affiliating with a provincial aristocratic family, he was presumably trying to strengthen ties to a vital part of the country. Ankhenesmerire II became the mother of Pepi II of the Sixth Dynasty, who was possibly history's longest lived monarch, reaching at least 100 years of age. The regency role Pepi's mother assumed during his minority is expressed by the alabaster statue of this pair now in Brooklyn, where the young king sits on his mother's knees. The wives of both Pepi I and II had their own pyramid complexes, imitating the kings in both architectural and textual details.

Their Sixth Dynasty ended the Old Kingdom period, which closed with the reign of a female pharaoh: Nitokerty who lived around 2200 B.C. (Zivie, 1982, 513-16). She was remembered in legend down to the very end of ancient Egyptian history (as related in both Herodotus and Manetho) as "the bravest and most beautiful woman of her time," but the story behind this reputation remains a mystery. She is alleged, by ancient historians, to have succeeded her murdered brother and then taken revenge upon his murderers by a clever plot. However, this may be merely a tale told to embellish a reign about which very little was remembered (Callendar, 1992, 27-29).

In all, at least five queens assumed the kingship during native dynasties and would have been proclaimed as the "Female Horus, the King of Upper and Lower Egypt, the Daughter of Re," but between the haphazard survival of evidence from remote times and deliberate political attacks which followed some of them, disappointingly little is known of most of these female pharaohs: Nitokerty, Sobekneferu, Hatshepsut, Nefertiti and Tawosret. The last three reigned during the New Kingdom, but Sobekneferu was an exception during the Middle Kingdom, reigning at the end of the Twelfth Dynasty.

The Twelfth Dynasty developed as one of the most energetic periods of Egyptian history with many ambitious building projects including great fortresses to protect Egypt's southern border and extensive irrigation projects to increase productivity in the fertile Fayum district in the north. Truly colossal images of the rulers were erected, and there survive a good number of pieces of statuary, smaller in scale, which commemorate the royal women of this dynasty, including the stunning head from a female sphinx, probably belonging to a princess, now in the collection of The Brooklyn Museum.

The royal pyramids of the time incorporated the burials of the royal women (king's mother, wife and daughters) and at times (for instance in the reign of Senusert III) these great monuments were exclusively the place of the royal women's burials, as that king appears to have had himself buried far away from his capital at the sacred cemetery site of Abydos. Both his mother, queen Khenemetneferhedjet Weret and his wife Neferethenut, were buried in the north, right under the pyramid at Dashur, and a vast catacomb of tombs of a dozen other royal women--daughters and sisters--are beneath the area to the north side of this pyramid (Arnold, 1995, 50). Happily the jewelry caches of several royal ladies of this family have been found, revealing many lovely creations in gold and inlaid semi-precious stones--tiaras, girdles, bracelets and pectorals. In addition, some of their sarcophagi contained stone maces and staffs such as would be expected with the burials of men (Cron, 1995, 39).

Queen Mereseger, the Great Royal Wife of Senusert III was honored with a cult, after her death, in the region of the Second Cataract, an area in which her husband had military campaigns and maintained eight fortresses. One scholar suggests that the queen may have accompanied Senusert on his tours there or may have been a native of the region herself (Van Siclen, 1992, 32).

One of ancient Egypt's greatest construction works, a real marvel of the ancient world, was the so-called Labyrinth situated next to the pyramid of Amenemhet III in the Fayum district at Hawara. When the famous archaeologist W. M. Flinders Petrie excavated its badly decayed ruins, he found evidence that the king's daughter Sobekneferu, was responsible for its construction, along with her father (Petrie 1912, 50-53). Certainly, she eventually inherited his throne, so she probably oversaw the completion of this huge temple complex, which would have required many years to build.

Sobekneferu ruled as a full-fledged king at the close of the Twelfth Dynasty and also erected other temples (as at Herakleopolis) and is responsible for a number of monuments throughout the country (Callender, 1992, 30). While ancient historians recorded the rule of such female pharaohs, modern historians have often passed over them or tried to question the legitimacy of one such as Sobekneferu, insinuating that she came to the throne by intrigue. The seven year reign of Amenemhet IV intervened between that of Amenemhet III and Sobekneferu in the Twelfth Dynasty, but, the fact that this woman was dutifully finishing her father's funerary monument, as a loyal heir would, and that the government did not collapse after her reign demonstrates the smooth transfer of power as well as the legitimacy of Sobekneferu's reign as pharaoh (Callender, 1992, 56).

It is from the memorials to certain queens left by later generations, the deification of some of them, and the use of their names by other queens and by commoners that the popularity and influence of a number of these Great Royal Wives shine through the mist of lost history. We do know that the queens had, not only a religious power base, but great wealth in the form of extensive estates, workshops, and their own palaces. The Great Royal Wife in effect lived apart from her husband and his harem of concubines and was, not only served by large staffs of servants, but had the services of some of the most prominent men of the realm as stewards, tutors and advisors. Pharaoh would have had to travel to his consort's palace and present himself there if he wished her company. As one male scholar (Redford, 1967, 72) has commented, "Here was matriliny and matrilocal residence with a vengeance!" Others have taken a different view and suggested that the queens had their own palaces so that the king could be more free to dally with his concubines or secondary wives. At any rate, the queens administered vast households with extensive farm lands and factories for the production of luxury products including jewelry, perfume, wigs, and fabrics.

### Concubines

While they are the most poorly documented, leaving few monuments behind them, concubines were probably one of the perquisites of the male kings throughout Egypt's history. The literary tale of jolly old king Snefru at the dawn of the Fourth Dynasty personally planning a boating expedition in which he is to be rowed on a lake by scantily attired maidens strongly suggests that many fair young women in the palace were not there to be ladies in waiting for the queen (Lichtheim, 1973, 216). The fact that Pepi I could marry two sisters simultaneously also shows that a plurality of wives, at least at the highest level, was not unheard of, and indeed is documentable for several reigns of the later New Kingdom period.

In the Middle Kingdom, the great funerary monument of the Eleventh Dynasty ruler Montuhotep II, constructed on the west bank of ancient Thebes at Deir el Bahari, contained not only his tomb, funerary temple and a temple to Hathor, but the graves and funerary shrines of half a dozen women bearing the title of royal wife and prophet of Hathor. A large number of other women with lesser titles also were buried here too. Amazingly, some of their mummies reveal successfully healed Cesarean sections. While this royal mausoleum is badly ruined, the finely decorated stone sarcophagi of some of the queens have survived (Naville, 1907, pls. 19-20; Saleh 1987, pls. 68-9).

Later centuries yield evidence of palaces for princesses and queens in the fertile Fayum district, an oasis like depression southwest of modern Cairo. The Eighteenth and Nineteenth Dynasty kings welcomed as brides the daughters of many Western Asiatic monarchs and these princesses came to Egypt with large retinues of servants and musicians. Housing these women must have required palaces supported by extensive estates. Besides agricultural holdings, the queens' palaces contained large weaving workshops that produced the clothing for the royal households and women were among the supervisors of this production (Wente, 1990, 36).

Although some of the king's ladies lived much of their lives away from the pharaoh, written evidence of several periods proves that the queen, princesses and secondary wives were not locked away out of sight, but appeared in public, as in the audience chamber of the king (Lichtheim, 1973, 232), participating in rituals at temples and at great national events like victory celebrations and royal jubilees (Epigraphic Survey, 1980, pls. 31-2).

Some royal wives were avid promoters of a son not in line for the throne. More than once, younger queens or concubines in the royal harem, became involved in court intrigues and attempted to alter the succession by assassination. Such conspiracies, where "women marshaled the ranks" are documented for the reigns of Amenemhet I of the Twelfth Dynasty (Lichtheim,1973, 137) and Ramses III of the Twentieth (Goedicke, 1954 & 1973).

That against Ramses III, is the best documented "harem" conspiracy: led by a lesser queen named Tiy involving influential men in government and palace life, several members of the royal harem, plus a number of people outside the palace walls including army officers. It is obvious that the royal concubines had easy access to their relatives, and communication with the outside world was not difficult for them. One woman urged her brother to stir up the populace in an insurrection to coincide with the plotting within the palace. Incidentally, the men who served and guarded the pharaoh's harem and assisted in this plot, were not eunuchs but married men (De Buck, 1937; Goedicke, 1973). It is quite possible that many more intrigues altered the course of Egyptian history than is indicated by surviving records.

## A Dynasty of Formidable Females

After more than a century, during which foreigners exerted political control over Egypt, a noble family from the Thebaid in Upper Egypt organized an effective opposition and succeeded with armed attacks in freeing Egypt and establishing the brilliant period known as the New Kingdom, a veritable golden age when Egypt's wealth and political influence increased as never before.

It is really not until this New Kingdom that monumental art and commemorative inscriptions begin to record more fully the deeds of specific royal women. Pharaoh Ahmose of the Eighteenth Dynasty (1554-1529 B.C.) exhorted all his subjects to pay reverence and homage to his mother, Queen Ahhotep, for her heroic role in freeing Egypt from humiliating foreign domination during the wars against the dynasty known to history as the Hyksos, who had been for about a century the over-lords of Egypt. Apparently, when the queen's first born son, Kamose, fell in battle, she rallied the Upper Egyptian soldiers to continue to fight the enemy and rid the land of them, in order to clear the way for her family from Upper Egypt to rule over a united kingdom once again (Redford, 1967, 69). The foreign dynasty had its power base in the Delta at a site called Avaris, where recent archaeological work has revealed hundreds of fragments of distinctively Aegean, if not Minoan, wall paintings connected with a large building of the Eighteenth Dynasty (Hankey, 1993; Bietak, 1995, 21). While this may indicate only cultural influence, the subsequent description of the first queen of the Egyptian Eighteenth Dynasty, Ahhotep, as "Mistress of the *Hau Nebu*" hints at Mediterranean island connections or possessions (Redford, 1967, 70).

Queen Ahhotep's burial surprised archaeologists with its richness and variety. A horde of jewelry and elegant weapons had been placed within her mummy wrappings. The jewelry included the military decoration of valor: golden flies (Saleh & Sourouzian, 1987, pls. 120-22). References to this queen's valor may be read on the great stela that her son King Ahmose set up at Karnak temple where he recalled: *"She cared for her soldiers...she brought back her fugitives and gathered up her deserters. she has pacified Upper Egypt and expelled her rebels"* (Breasted, 1906, 29-32).

Pharaoh Ahmose's wife was also extraordinary, as her subsequent deification and cult among the common people, which survived her by many centuries, testifies. This Queen Ahmose-Nefertari is credited with taking the lead in restoring the temples and official cults throughout the land after decades of neglect during the Hyksos period (Gitton, 1975, 32). In Thebes, the great religious center and home of the King of the Gods, she controlled the position of Second Prophet in his cult at Karnak. She then sold the position to her husband in exchange for an endowment to support a college of Divine Votaresses. The queen herself was a high priestess and overseer of this order of temple women, as her title of God's Wife of Amun testifies. She outlived her husband and was regent and advisor for her son, Amenhotep I. Ahmose-Nefertari's title "Female Chieftain of Upper and Lower Egypt," which seems to be unique, probably dates from the time she was regent for her son for seven years. Still another of her titles dated back to certain Old Kingdom queens: "the one who says all things and they are done for her." When she died, the dowager queen was provided with a coffin many times her size: twelve feet long and fitted with the lofty plumed crown of the God's Wife. Because of its height and its headdress (a very unusual feature for a mummy case), it is likely that the coffin was kept upright for a period of time and was viewed by many of the great queen's subjects, perhaps as her mummy made a post-mortem pilgrimage by river boat to the holy city of Abydos, sacred to Osiris, where the queens of her family had cenotaphs. Her cult, centering on a mortuary temple dedicated to her alone on the west bank at Thebes, was celebrated in many smaller local shrines erected around the country by her subjects for centuries afterwards. In these cult places the deified queen was often associated with her son, Amenhotep I. Unlike her husband and son, this queen was sometimes portrayed by later generations as having been black, although her coffin portrait gives her the typical light yellow skin of women.

### Hatshepsut

The granddaughter of Aḥmose-Nefertari, the great ruler Hatshepsut, arrogated the sovereignty of Egypt to herself after the reign of her husband (the son of a royal concubine). She was the sole surviving child of the mighty warrior-king Thutmose I and his Great Royal wife. Undoubtedly Hatshepsut felt that her credentials to rule as king were of the best and to reach her goal she must have arranged for the support of the oracle of the King of the Gods, as we know she had the backing of the high priest of Amun-Re as well as other powerful men of her father's court. Hatshepsut recorded that at her coronation she was instructed by the god: *"You shall seize the chiefs of Retenu by violence, those left over from your father('s reign); your catch shall be men by the thousands for the temples."*

Today the visitor to her temple at Deir el-Bahri, on the west bank at Luxor, finds that the lowest colonnade at ground level has sustained the worst damage. There is extensive and deliberate erasure of most of its wall inscriptions, surely occasioned by their historical nature. Here the first foreign war campaign of her father, Thutmose I, is cited as a precedent for Hatshepsut's first war campaign into Nubia. Unfortunately there are now numerous gaps in the many lines of text, but phrases like "a slaughter was made among them;" "horses upon the mountains;" "she has destroyed the southern lands;" indicate the story of the female pharaoh's victories was the subject (Redford, 1967, 59).

The Great female pharaoh, Hatshepsut
Photo courtesy Metropolitan Museum
of Art, New York

The deliberate erasure of such texts has always been taken by Egyptologists as indicating that Hatshepsut's immediate successor, Thutmose III, did not want any remembrance of the effective leadership of his step mother to remain with her subjects. However there are other private records from the memorials of at least three prominent men of Hatshepsut's reign which demonstrate the truth of her claims (Habachi, 1957, 99-101). That her reign also launched a campaign to the east into Asia and subdued Gaza, probably repeating the achievement of her father and his predecessor, may not indicate the queen herself was present then, but underlines the fact that her foreign policy was not one of benign neglect or pacivity as some earlier historians have interpreted. In all there were at least four war campaigns during Hatshepsut's tenure, but Thutmose III may have conducted the later ones as he was then of an age to do this and the pharaoh trusted him as co-regent with control of the army.

Hatshepsut was an anomaly. Very few female pharaohs ruled during Egypt's three thousand years of ancient history. However, she was far from being an usurper. No one would have questioned her right and duty to rule the country as regent for a minor. No one seems to have opposed her consequent claim to a more independent rule either, so it is surprising that her very strong and accomplished successor should have felt it necessary to eradicate her memory. One can only speculate on what disasters or conspiracies might have threatened Egypt during his reign to persuade him (or his priesthood) to take such dire steps against the spirit of the female pharaoh.

Hatshepsut enjoyed a long reign over the most powerful nation in the world of her time. Her brilliant rule was marked by prosperity exemplified by the resumption of long distance trade, -- for example, with the far off land of Punt (Eritrea) on the Red Sea coast, from which Egyptians obtained frankincense and myrrh used in temple ritual.

Hatshepsut was one of the great builders of Egypt's history. Starting early in her career, she began work at her mortuary temple against the western cliffs at Thebes and also across the river at Karnak, the seat of the king of the gods, where she renovated earlier structures and erected a new sanctuary for the sacred boat shrine of Amun-Re. She also built a series of new rooms depicting her as offering before various gods. Most spectacularly, she placed two gigantic obelisks at the eastern side of the main temple, the largest known up to that time, and entirely covered them with a thin gold sheet. These were toppled and reused as building stone by her successor, but Hatshepsut's other pair, erected between the 4th and 5th pylons of her father still stand. Although somewhat smaller they are still 29.5 meters in height and weigh 323 tons each (Habachi 1977, 60). She also began the monumental southern axis of the great temple by constructing what is called today Karnak's 8th pylon gateway.

There is reason to believe that Hatshepsut began construction of the sacred complex at Karnak dedicated to the goddess Mut, consort of Amun-Re and Lady of the Crowns. This goddess appears, in the sculpture of the New

Kingdom, wearing the double crown of Egypt, just as Hatshepsut would have herself. The female pharaoh also built a temple across the river at Medinet Habu and far north at Speos Artemidos and as far south as Aswan, but her greatest memorial, the greatest monument to a woman to survive from all antiquity, was her mortuary temple of Djeser-djeseru. Its unique design is thought to have been the inspiration of the Royal Steward, Senenmut. This magnificent terraced temple at Deir el-Bahri blends well with the impressive curtain of cliffs soaring behind it (Winlock, 1942; Wysocki, 1986). There were many old temples which needed repairs and refurbishing as well and Hatshepsut saw that this was done. The following inscription from Speos Artemidos expresses her pride in her mighty and pious deeds and in the gods' support of her.

> The temple of the Mistress of Kusae (Hathor), was fallen into ruin, and the earth had swallowed its august sanctuary while children danced on its roof. The serpent goddess no longer promoted terror, and ...its festivals no longer appeared. I sanctified it after it had been built anew. It is in order to protect her city that I fashioned her image from gold, with a barque for a land procession...
>
> Hear you, all patricians and all commoners as many as you are, I have done this by the plan of my heart. I can not sleep as a lowly one. I made to flourish what was ruined. I raised up what was cut up formerly since the Asiatics were in the fold of the Delta at Avaris, with foreigners in their midst overthrowing what had been made. Unmindful of Re they ruled, and he did not act by divine command down to (the time of) my majesty, I having been established on the thrones of Re. I was foretold for an a eternity of years as "she will become a conqueror." I have come as the Sole one of Horus flaming against my enemies. I have removed the abomination of the gods, and the earth had brought away their footprints. This was the instruction of the father of my fathers who came at his appointed times, Re. "Never shall occur the destruction of what Amun had commanded." My command is firm like the mountains and the disk shines and spreads rays over the titulary of my majesty, and my falcon is high over the serekh forever and ever. (Gardiner 1946; L. H. Lesko translation).

Hatshepsut originally intended her daughter Neferure to succeed her as Pharaoh, and provided her with a very cultured male courtier as a tutor and steward. This was Hatshepsut's favorite: Senenmut who was Chief of All Works and held a host of other titles under the pharaoh, the most lucrative of which was probably Chief Steward of the Estate of Amun-Re, King of the Gods. A man of humble origin, his meteoric rise in wealth and power is demonstrated by the fact that his father was buried without mummification in a simple grave while his mother, who lived longer, was buried by Senenmut in a sarcophagus, mummified and provided with all the paraphernalia of a proper elite Egyptian burial, and laid to rest in a tomb Senenmut constructed for his family.

The pride that this man took in his important relationship with Hatshepsut's daughter the princess Neferure is reflected by the numerous sculptured portraits of himself holding the young girl (Dorman, 1988, 220-21). On these he boasts of raising the princess, which shows probably that she was not being brought up to assume a typically feminine role but probably the rulership, after her mother.  Senenmut was granted (or took) many opportunities to memorialize himself, not only in statues but by inserting his name and image on the monuments of his pharaoh, as in her mortuary temple at Deir el Bahri. His burial chamber was constructed within her temple's precinct, and his sarcophagus was of the royal style.  Because he never married, some have linked Senenmut and Hatshepsut romantically, but without any evidence one can only speculate about this and also about why Senenmut was never buried in either of his tombs and why his sarcophagus was smashed into 1400 fragments.  His "fall" cannot, unfortunately, even be dated with assurance (Dorman, 1988, 180).

Unfortunately, Hatshepsut suffered other disappointments.  Neferure died young, and her mother had to bow to political necessity and designate the previously deposed step-son Thutmose III as her heir.  She allowed him full control of the army and had him portrayed with her on the walls of the monuments which she erected during the latter part of her reign.  Thus it is especially disappointing to find, many years after her death, that Thutmose III, though he had developed into a successful warrior-king, still felt the need to attempt to destroy the historical memory of the female pharaoh.  That his actions did not totally eradicate Hatshepsut's memory is shown by the fact that the Egyptian historian Manetho, writing a history in the Ptolemaic Period more than a thousand years later, using preserved official records, mentioned a 21 year reign for a woman ruler in the early Eighteenth Dynasty.

### Meryetre-Hatshepsut

Thutmose III is credited with creating the greatest empire the pharaohs ever possessed, establishing Egyptian control over coastal Palestine, the Levant and Syria as far as the Euphrates river to the borders of the Hurrian kingdom of Mitanni and as far south into the Sudan as the Fourth Cataract.  Although the tomb of three foreign wives of Thutmose III has been found at Thebes, that of his chief queen Meryetre-Hatshepsut has not surfaced yet.  However, this woman had a long life and, judging from her prominence in the monuments of her son's reign, appears to have been a major figure at the court of Amenhotep II (1425-1401 B.C.), whom she apparently outlived (Van Siclen, 1995, 168).  She retained the title Great Royal Wife during her son's reign and had a tomb prepared for herself in the Valley of the Kings.  Later, however, in the reign of his successor, Thutmose IV, her monumental references were usurped by his queen Tiaa and the dowager queen's tomb was handed over to the use of others. Obviously palace intrigues were rife at the court of the pharaohs, and women, who were ambitious for themselves as well as for their own sons, were probably often at their center.

## Tiy

The following reign of Amenhotep III, often called Amenhotep the Magnificent (Kozloff, 1992) for the high quality of art and the extent of his monumental building, introduces another remarkable woman. Tiy was the daughter of highly placed courtiers, but still a commoner in comparison to the divine pharaoh. Amenhotep III distributed copies of a marriage commemorative scarab throughout his vast realm to celebrate this marriage and the affectionate king also caused his wife to be portrayed together with him in equally colossal size in monumental statuary groups.

Queen Tiy is found portrayed in sculpture as the earthly manifestation of the goddess Hathor, was identified as such in her own temple at Sedeinga, and was worshipped also as the goddesses Tefnut, Isis, Mut, Maat, Taweret and Sekhmet, thus spanning many important features from fertility to divine protection and justice. Elsewhere she was portrayed as a sphinx trampling the enemies of Egypt, although theirs was a very peaceful reign (Morkot, 1986). Contemporary records acknowledge Tiy as interested in foreign affairs and in matters of state (Moran, 1987, 84-92). On occasion she corresponded with foreign rulers such as the king of Mitanni, in what is now Syria, at this time Egypt's chief ally against the Anatolian Hittites. Tiy bore Amenhotep at least six children, four girls and two boys. The eldest daughter, Princess Sit-Amun enjoyed her own independent existence, upon maturity, in a palace of her own. The next eldest daughter, Princess Henuttaneb, may well have carried out the role of God's wife of Amun in this reign as she appears as the central figure in the gigantic family group statue now in the atrium of the Cairo Museum where

---

**The Marriage Scarab of Amenhotep III and Tiy**

*Live The Horus: "the Strong Bull, appearing in Truth,"*

*The Two Ladies: "the Establisher of Laws, the Pacifier of the Two Lands."*

*The Horus of Gold: "Great Falchion, who smites the Asiatics,"*

*The King of Upper and Lower Egypt: "Neb-maa-Re,"*

*The Son of Re: "Amenhotep, ruler of Thebes," given life.*

*And may the Chief Royal Wife, Tiy, live. The name of her father is*

*Yuya, the name of her mother is Tuya.*

*She is the wife of the mighty king,*

*whose southern boundary is at Karoy*

*whose northern boundary is at Naharin.*

her headdress has a socket for the addition of the double plumes of gold associated with this rank. Amenhotep was offered foreign princesses for purposes of sealing friendly diplomatic relations in the Middle East of that time, and his harem palaces--filled with the large retinues of such for wives--must have helped set the very cosmopolitan and sophisticated tone for this period. Although requested, Pharaoh Amenhotep never allowed any of his own daughters to be sent away to a foreign court in marriage, instead finding a woman of lesser rank to satisfy the foreign potentate.

Nefertiti at the altar of the god Aton whose rays shine down upon her. From recently recovered blocks of the destroyed temple to the Aton at Karnak.

Courtesy of Donald B. Redford

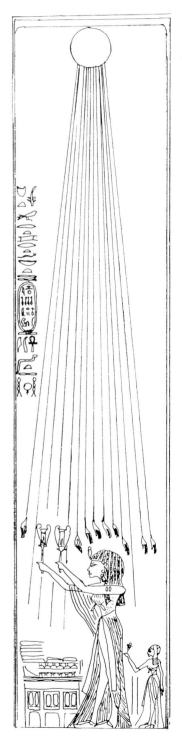

## Nefertiti

Queen Tiy outlived her husband and was able to visit their eldest surviving son in his new capital city in the twelfth year of his reign. By that time Pharaoh Amenhotep IV had changed his name to Akhenaten (probably Akhaniaty would be more correct) and, through his radical departures with tradition in religion, art, and government, had guaranteed himself history's label as the "heretic pharaoh." We have few details about the background of his Great Royal Wife Nefertiti, but she too was probably the daughter of highly-placed courtiers, possibly the same family as Tiy's (Grimal, 1992, 226). Her name means "the beautiful woman has come," and her life-sized portrait bust speaks eloquently of ageless beauty as well as intelligence and queenly assurance. The portrait was executed in accordance with the naturalistic style of the unconventional art of this reign, but the queen was also portrayed in unusual contexts on other monuments. First of all, she and her daughters (six are known) were exposed to unprecedented publicity. They were depicted in hundreds of scenes at worship, on the reviewing stand, and even as they lived within the palace. Most unusual, intimate scenes of family togetherness and affection became standard in the repertoire of the state artists.

Many portrayals of Nefertiti indicate her prominent role in the new religion promulgated by Akhenaten. This was a monotheistic-type worship of the solar disk, the Aten. Sometimes Nefertiti alone, or with her eldest daughter, was shown at the altar of her god in the sanctuary built to him at Karnak in the early years of the reign. In other places, the entire family was portrayed as worshipping together at the open-air altars of the sun disk, but the court and populace were encouraged to address their prayers for long life, success and other intentions to the royal couple rather than directly to the Aten.

Despite his closeness to Nefertiti, the king had more than one wife, having inherited a harem of foreign and Egyptian ladies from his father. Probably because Nefertiti bore him six daughters but no son, he had another queen, one Kiya, but she appears to have died young, and her name was erased from the monuments, replaced by those of Nefertiti's daughters (Helck, 1980, 422-24).

Indeed the sense of equality of power between Akhenaten and his Great Royal Wife comes through most strongly in the religious texts of this period. Nefertiti appended before her name that of Neferneferuaten "Beautiful is the Beauty of the Aten" and the name of the god always is written so as to face Nefertiti as if to indicate clearly their very close affiliation. Signs of the unusual prominence of Nefertiti have been found in the iconography of the reign as well. As with Queen Tiy, vignettes depicted Nefertiti as only pharaohs had been portrayed in previous centuries. Sometimes she is shown wearing a true pharaoh's crown--the blue helmet favored by kings of the New Kingdom--and standing, not to the left, but to the right of her husband in sculpture groups where they were depicted in equal dimensions. Sometimes she wields a scimitar, in an exclusively pharaonic pose (Morkot, 1986; B. Lesko, 1991).

Pharaoh Akhenaton, Nefertiti and their baby girls. After a relief in the Ägyptisches Museum, Berlin.

What does this mean? Was Nefertiti only the high priestess of a revolutionary religion that denied the existence of all gods other than the solar aspects of the one all-encompassing Deity? Was she regarded as a goddess herself? Did she actually share and later assume the rulership of Egypt upon the death or incapacitation of her sickly husband as some scholars have recently come to suspect? Some have speculated that Nefertiti is none other than the pharaoh Smenkhkare who reigned briefly after Akhenaten and just before Tutankhamun. It has also been suggested that she was an interim ruler between Akhenaten and Smenkhkare. The likelihood that Nefertiti did rule as king for a time is widely accepted among Egyptologists (Allen, 1994). Interestingly, the presence of a woman monarch in the late Eighteenth Dynasty was still recalled by Manetho one thousand years later.

### Ankhesenamun

One of Nefertiti's daughters was Ankhesenamun, the bride of Pharaoh Tutankhamun. While she was portrayed on the artifacts found in the famous

Tutankhamun and Ankhesenamun from the panel of an inlaid chest found in his tomb. Permission to reproduce photo courtesy of the Egyptian Museum, Cairo.

tomb as a charming and devoted young wife whose world was centered upon her husband, the historical facts show she too was a strong woman true to her line. Once widowed, her ambition seems to have known no bounds. Ankhesenamun appears to have been determined to hold the throne for herself at any cost, even if it required the unheard of act of taking as a partner a foreign prince (no more young and royal men being available to her in Egypt, no others being deemed worthy apparently). Not only did she apply for the hand of a foreign prince, but she sought one from the enemy's side! All we know for certain is that a female member and widowed queen of Akhenaten's family wrote to the king of the Hittite Empire requesting one of his sons as her husband (Goetze, 1955, 319). Needless to say, the possibility of so easily consolidating the Hittite and Egyptian realms into a single mighty world-empire must have exceeded the dreams of the ambitious Hittite ruler. At first incredulous, he finally agreed. However, saner minds prevailed on the Nile. We know the hapless prince died on his approach to Egypt. History tells no more of Ankhesenamun, but her figure has been almost completely obliterated from the side of her husband's colossal statue now in Chicago's Oriental Institute Museum (and on its twin in Cairo). Nefertiti, Ankhesenamun and their husbands were stricken from the official records and their buildings and other monuments were destroyed by those who followed them to power in Egypt. It is only because of the archaeological and philological work of the Twentieth Century that anything is known about these remarkable people.

### Mutnodjme

The generalissimo Haremheb, whose reign ended the Eighteenth Dynasty, married the sister of Nefertiti in an attempt to gain legitimacy for his coup, as he was not of royal blood. He then undertook to bring order to a realm that had been plunged into disorder due to the lax leadership of his predecessors. In a great edict concerning his law and order policies, it is stated that the agents of the queen and the scribes of the table in the harem had for years been collecting taxes (Kruchten,1981,196). Haremheb reacted against this negatively, but the fact suggests that the queen in the Eighteenth Dynasty, at least, was the head of an administration that not only received but collected revenues and that her duties were far from limited to the ceremonial or religious. The probability of this is underscored by the fact that a number of royal women ruled over Egypt, whether as regents for an under-aged son or as a female pharaoh and could not easily have handled such extensive responsibilities if they had never known any. In a sense, the queen as Mistress of All Women and Lady of the Two Lands occupied a position in the kingdom much like numerous women of property (who bore the title Mistress of the Household) did on the private level, overseeing the receiving and storing of their estate produce and commanding the domestic servants.

The smaller temple of Abu Simbel dedicated to Queen Nefertari and the goddess Hathor.

### Nefertari

In subsequent dynasties, Egypt was ruled by other families, and little can be gleaned from the records about the personalities of their women, even though the tombs of a number of them survive. The mother of Ramses II, the wife of Seti I of the Nineteenth Dynasty, was honored by her son with a funerary temple and a stunning colossal statue, a twelve foot high portrait of herself now in the Vatican. She and the chief consorts of her long-reigned son were given elaborate tombs in the Valley of the Queens, adjacent to the valley containing the tombs of the kings of the New Kingdom. The most beautifully decorated of these to survive belonged to the first queen of Ramses II, Nefertari-Merymut. Here, as in other queen's tombs, the Great Royal Wife is shown in the company of the major deities, but one may look in vain for any mention of the king, whose name and figure do not appear in the tomb, although they are found in the tombs of royal princes. The great ladies were able to join the gods of the afterworld strictly on their own merits.

This same Queen Nefertari, who predeceased her long-lived spouse, was honored as well with the hewing of a magnificent monument in Nubia: the smaller of the two rock-cut temples at Abu Simbel where colossal statues of the queen alternate with those of her husband across the imposing facade of the temple dedicated to her and Hathor, the goddess with whom she was identified. Years later the 31 foot tall colossal statue of her daughter Meritamun would stand beside that of her royal father at a temple he had built in the city of Akhmim in middle Egypt, surely one of the tallest statues ever created of a living woman.

## Tawosret

The very long reign of Ramses II dominates the history of the Nineteenth Dynasty. Following his sixty-seven years on the throne, Egypt was badly in need of young and dynamic leadership which, unfortunately, she did not get. Instead the country was racked by serious dynastic crises, even though Ramses II had engendered dozens of sons. In the end, the last legitimate member of the royal dynastic family, Queen Tawosret, took up the challenge of governing and became Pharaoh under the throne name of Sit-Re 'daughter of Re." She ruled long enough to sponsor expeditions in Sinai and Palestine and to begin building projects which included a mortuary temple and a large royal tomb excavated for herself in the Valley of the Kings at Thebes. Again Manetho recalled in his chronicle a female pharaoh ending this dynasty, but details of Tawosret's reign are very sparse (L. Lesko, 1966).

The rulers of the Old and New Kingdoms were the most powerful monarchs in the world at their time, so it is gratifying to find women on the throne as pharaohs. However, they were few in number and often were attacked politically after their reigns. It is significant, however, that the Greco-Egyptian Manetho, who compiled historical recollections in the third century B.C. did have at his command records of the existence of female rulers showing that the attempted eradication of their memory was not totally successful. The queens who were honored by later generations were those who had accepted responsibility in periods of instability when few men would have welcomed the task.

Statue of Yuny and Rennutet, Dynasty
19, MMA 15.2.1. (Rogers Fund, 1915).
    Courtesy of the Metropolitan
Museum of Art, New York

# THE AVERAGE WOMAN

*"The Egyptians themselves in their manners and customs seem to have reversed the ordinary practices of mankind. For instance, women attend market and are employed in trade, while men stay at home and do the weaving."*

Herodotus *Histories,*
Book II, 35

Why should Herodotus, the so-called "father of history" who traveled to Egypt in the mid Fifth Century B.C., have been so struck by the oddity of seeing women in public? What is so extraordinary about women shopping or being merchants? The answer lies in the observer's background. Herodotus was a Greek, and in Fifth Century Greece, even in the enlightened city of Athens, married women were very much confined to their homes; nearly all forms of outdoor recreation were closed to them; and men were viewed as the only ones properly suited for activities outside the home in the greater society. That is why the Greek men frequented the market place, and indeed the Agora was the center of Greek civilized life, where the male citizens met to exchange gossip and political and philosophical viewpoints. As we see from the poetry of Sappho and the plays of Euripides, Greek girls were married at an early age to men they did not know in arranged marriages and paid a rich dowry for the honor. They generally received no physical or mental training, but were taught only homemaking skills like cooking and weaving and were expected to keep quiet and modest. Not until the Fourth Century B.C. did intelligent men in Greece begin discussing the advantages of extending some training in music and dance to women. But even Socrates did not conceive of careers for them.

Lady merchant from a market place. Scene in the tomb of Ken-Amon Mayor of Thebes, reign of Amen-hotep III.

Line drawing by Susan Weeks.

Such patriarchal attitudes were not unique to ancient Greece, of course. All civilized societies known from history have been male dominated, including our own. Extreme forms of patriarchy are found in the laws and literature of many of the earliest Near Eastern societies--such as the Babylonians and Assyrians--and through biblical stories and their interpretations (or misinterpretations) have influenced many of the world's peoples ever since. That is why it is fascinating to confront the evidence from ancient Egypt, where as far back as 2700 B.C. legal equality existed between the sexes and women were not confined to their homes but had a "public life" as well. This is an important fact, as the contrary has been vigorously argued by influential feminists such as Simone de Beauvoir, whose book *The Second Sex,* although written before serious research on early women had begun, has had enormous influence world wide. It is only by carefully examining as much source material as possible from the earliest of civilizations that a more accurate women's story can be reconstructed.

Fortunately, the field of women's studies is expanding rapidly as a university discipline which spans many fields--anthropology, literature, and history are but the most obvious. The combined efforts of researchers are continually bringing into focus clearer images of women's roles in the development of civilization and their findings are proving that there have been many misconceptions and misunderstandings of women's lives through the ages. Biases of earlier researchers and awareness of our own prejudices need to be kept in mind when conducting such research.

Two servant statues from tombs of the Old Kingdom at Giza. Woman brewer and woman grinding grain, Numbers. 6-19811 and 6-19766 respectively. Courtesy of the P.A. Hearst Museum of Anthropology University of California, Berkeley.

# Public Life / Private Life

### Equal under the law:

Both women and men had identical legal status in ancient Egypt with all the responsibilities as well as advantages this entailed. This situation can be traced back to the Third Dynasty, or about 2700 B.C. Women, like men, were able to own, purchase, inherit or dispose of their property--both real estate and objects. Women entered into contracts themselves, never requiring a legal co-signatory or guardian. This more than anything demonstrates their legal independence in the eyes of the state, an independence Egyptian women seem to have enjoyed from earliest times and throughout pharaonic history. The importance of this fact is obvious to any reader who is old enough to recall the laws of the United States of America as late as the middle of the Twentieth Century A.D.!

Law and justice in the Egyptian State emanated from Pharaoh, but they were not rigid and seem to have lacked some consistency especially with regard to civil rights. The status of the native-born Egyptian citizen changed over the course of millennia in the direction of increasing freedom and opportunity, in both this life and the next, for those whom one might call "average" or "middle class." Into this category would fit common-born people who were skilled craftsmen, scribes, soldiers, and stable masters, farmers, beekeepers and herdsmen. In the New Kingdom all these people were able to own land and slaves and were free to pass on their property to their heirs. How much freedom they had to change jobs or places of residence is not clear, but that they could rise in status through their proven abilities is certain from the records kept by the families of artists, sculptors and scribes. It can also be stated with confidence that the wives and daughters of these men enjoyed similar status and legal rights.

As independent legal entities, women could take oaths, witness documents such as wills and contracts, and give testimony in court. They might buy and free slaves, adopt children and sue (even her own father in one case from c. 1780 B.C.). Daughters shared inheritances. Occasionally they sat on juries and served as executrixes of estates too. However, equality of the sexes meant there was no difference in the treatment women received from the state or before a tribunal. Thus women, like men, when called before judges were often questioned under torture: being beaten with the stick or having their hands and feet twisted to encourage them to speak truthfully (Peet, 1930, 148-52).

The participation of women in the national service (or State *Corvée*) more than anything else demonstrates the official view that women and men were of equal worth, were equally obligated as subjects, and were equally capable of rendering useful service to the nation. Officially, the view was that "women's place" was *not* only in the home. National service, for which every citizen was theoretically liable unless given a personal exemption from the king, was the means the ruler had of calling up sufficient hands--in this pre industrial age--for building and repairing dikes, moving huge building stones from quarries to construction sites, and even for defending the borders (Hayes, 1955, 29). Women were not excluded from national service, and while work on the dikes and cooking for the construction teams might be assigned some, others were set to work in the weaving studios producing the linen fabric used by the Egyptians as a primary medium of exchange as well as a means of clothing workers and propelling sailing vessels.

Such labor for the state was a way for non land-working people to pay their taxes. Anyone trying to escape would be apprehended and, if not, her family could be taken hostage against her return (Hayes, 1955, 64-5). Farming families paid over a percentage of their harvest and then, if family members were called up for service during the long annual flood season, they were paid from the same grain stores the state had collected as taxes. Thus the wealth of the nation was recycled and the population of ancient Egypt was kept fed, busy, and productive. As a result, the gross national product of Egypt must have been far greater than any of its contemporaries. The Nile valley's fertility was impressive and its natural resources included gold, copper, turquoise and other semi-precious stones and excellent building stone as well. Surrounded by less sophisticated neighbors, the large and urban population of Egypt enjoyed a physical security which was a rare luxury in antiquity. Indeed, the security felt by this people may be a major factor explaining the liberal attitude demonstrated toward women (B. Lesko, 1987, 74).

## Women in the work force:

Tomb wall scenes, which reflect aspects of life on the estate and in the workplace of the owner, tended in all periods to show far less of women's activities than men's. Thus texts and other types of art, like statuary, have to be examined too. Not long ago, a statue was discovered of a servant woman grinding pigments for a painter even though tomb scenes of artisan workshops never include women (Hawass 1992, 242). Occasionally tombs from the third and second millennia depict women buying and selling in the market place, showing that at least some Egyptian women contributed to their household's wealth and also had purchasing power. Considering Herodotus's comment of centuries later, this remained a feature of Egyptian life although it was not a feature common to all ancient societies. The women in the market stalls probably manufactured their stock of sandals, baskets, and beverages or had grown the produce they were selling. However, their freedom to participate in the open market place did not necessarily convey much prestige, as even male traders seem not to have been given any type of high social standing in Egypt (Kemp, 1991, 257). Other women are shown in tomb scenes doing surprising things like piloting boats (Fischer, 1989, figs. 9 & 10).

Pottery is a female craft most places in Africa, and yet is not depicted in the Egyptian tomb paintings as such. However those scenes have been recognized as depicting relatively few aspects of Egyptian life (B. Lesko, 1989, 117), and there may well have been many more activities open to women than the scenes portray. Both artistic and written documentation indicates that weaving was a prime occupation of women and, in the beginning, totally her own. Men do not seem to have become involved until the Empire period when the technology developed a different type of standing loom. Linen cloth was a prime commodity of exchange in this barter economy. Thus a talented woman, especially a deft weaver and seamstress, could enhance her family's wealth considerably (B. Lesko, 1994, 37). Economic documents are rare, but the accounts of a large Middle Kingdom household show the senior female members receiving the same pay rations as the men in the family (Wente, 1990, 61).

Women spinners and weavers from tomb number 2 at El Bersheh, Middle Kingdom.
Line drawing by Susan Weeks.

At the upper end of the social scale, we find a female overseer of female physicians (Harer, 1989, 960-61). Written sources yield other titles of women in supervisory positions in commerce and industry such as "Mistress of the Wig Workshop" or "Mistress of the Dining Hall," or "Overseer of Weavers." Also recorded are positions for women in the palace such as Overseers of Dancing for the King, Inspector of the Treasure, and Steward of the Queen (Ward, 1986, 3-23). Most significant, as it indicates the great trust placed in the women office holders, are the "treasurers" and "sealers" who managed the accumulated goods of the families they served. These women are testified to in late Old Kingdom and Middle Kingdom sources from around the country (Callender, 1992, 14; Ward, 1986).

Tombs of the Old Kingdom aristocracy exhibit scenes of women being rewarded with precious jewelry by the state (Nord, 1970). This may have been for their productivity in weaving linen as the state and temples had their own factories to produce luxuries for the royal family and gods. Women staffed these, producing some of the finest linen cambric ever manufactured: 200 threads to the inch and almost transparent with the texture of silk. While the paintings from the religious context of tombs show Egyptians favoring plain white linen clothing, this may be an indication of the ritual purity of the deceased and those in the funeral ceremonies. Colorful garments are portrayed on wooden statues of women, and from tombs have come examples of embroidery, beaded, and sequin-decorated accessories for both sexes. Houses and boats were accented with colorful fabrics of intricate designs too.

There are two letters which have survived from the Old Kingdom and the New Kingdom from women administrators of royal weaving workshops. The later one, sent to the Pharaoh Seti II, recalls a long career dating back to his grandfather's reign and the training that the woman correspondent had given to talented foreign workers (Wente, 1990, 36).

Fragrant oils and perfumes were a necessity for both men and women in the hot, dry climate of Egypt--hence the importance of this industry. Like the textile factories, the perfume houses often were associated with the estates of the Great Royal Wife, those in the area near the Fayum lake in particular. Teams of women picked and pressed lilies to extract their essences. The fragrances extracted were added to oils used to rub into the skin after bathing and were also used in temple rites. Even statues of gods were anointed in the daily temple ritual, and the fragrant oils were so sought after and valuable that they are generally among the precious items recorded as stolen by ancient tomb robbers.

While women could hold jobs outside the home and even trained and administered staffs of workers, women rarely held positions in the governing bureaucracy. Only in the feudal age of the Middle Kingdom do a few women bear the titles suggesting they were rulers of cities (Millard, 1976, II, 268-271). However it is also clear that the right to the governing of provinces could

Women picking and pressing lilies from the Thirtieth Dynasty tomb of Pa-ir-kap in Heliopolis. Permission to reproduce courtesy of the Louvre, Paris.

descend from a mother to her son, if the mother was the only surviving heir of a governor. Some Middle Kingdom women have been found buried with staffs, maces, and scepters, similar to the king's flail, which was a short staff with three strings of beads attached (Mace, 1916, 76-103). This surely was a symbol of authority, and the women who possessed such a scepter were the relatives of men who enjoyed great social status and wealth. Such aristocratic women have also been portrayed in tombs and on stelae carrying staffs with lotus or papyrus heads, which may be a feminizing decoration to distinguish their staffs from those of their husbands. As the staff was a mark of authority, it is clear that women intimately associated with men of importance gained thereby for themselves. While sons might gain in wealth or political influence through their mother's side of the family, a woman born to high ranking parents, such as a princess, could stand to lose prestige upon marrying a man of lesser rank, as sometimes happened. Interestingly, women are mentioned among the enemies of the state in Middle Kingdom execration texts, thus suggesting that some were at times politically involved. This is obvious in the palace, where royal concubines sometimes promoted their son's advancement to the throne by violent means.

It is sometimes stated that, with the reign of Amenemhet III of the Twelfth Dynasty, more status was conveyed upon women because the title Mistress of the Household now appears for the first time (Malaise, 1977, 193). This probably denoted women of property, not marital status, although the two were usually coincidental.

The deity of writing was a goddess, Sheshat, and the appearance of the title scribess on documents of the Middle Kingdom indicates that, although literacy was not widespread, some women did learn to read and write and earned their living with these skills. Very likely those who did were the daughters of scribes because that class usually passed its positions along from generation to generation within its ranks and felt its profession and life style to be superior to all others. An ancient teacher advised his pupils:

Seshat the goddess of writing

*"As for writing, to the one who learns it, it is more profitable than any other office; it is more pleasing than bread and beer, more than clothing, more than ointment. It is more precious than an inheritance in Egypt, and worth more than a tomb on the Western Side "* (Pap. Lansing, BM 9994)

During the expanding empire of the New Kingdom, when the demand for educated leaders and a larger civil service increased, educational opportunities increased also, and there are indications that some women of the leisure class studied writing and probably learned to read the short stories and poetry of the time (Bryan, 1984). This does not mean they used such skills in jobs. Women seem to have been excluded from the government bureaucracy, partly because their vital role in perpetuation of the family was regarded of utmost importance in antiquity. Marriage was thus deemed preferable for girls to the lengthy training necessary for proficiency in writing and mathematics, skills demanded of the elite workforce of the civil administration. Life in a pre industrial society was arduous, of course. A family's survival depended on the skills of the women of the household, and they toiled long hours to prepare both clothing and food from scratch, with no labor saving devices at all accept for the servants found in the wealthier households.

Among the household servants, women tended to outnumber men considerably. This is probably due to men being used out of doors on the agricultural land and in building projects to a much greater extent than women, who had numerous chores within the house. Skilled weavers were always in demand, but the slave women who were controlled by the state and loaned out to the families of the civil servants who hewed and decorated the royal tombs were put to arduous tasks like the grinding of grain (J. Černý, 1973, 104-5; B. Lesko, 1994, 26). Children, both boys and girls, tended cattle, looked after younger children, and helped their parents in other ways. Sons were often trained at the side of their father to assume the same or similar job upon maturity, just as daughters learned by assisting their mothers. Roles were definitely determined by gender.

Young women had to be trained in the many and varied domestic arts required of a homemaker, whether the brewing of beer or the baking of bread or raising of crops. At a time when the average housewife had to weave the cloth before she could sew clothes for her family, she might first have had to learn the almost two dozen separate steps involved in turning flax into linen. Thus when we today say that ancient Egyptian women were not generally educated it is *we* who are making appraisals using standards biased by our own experiences and values.

While the male artists of the tomb paintings rarely depict the tasks of women, occasionally they show girls trapping birds and laboring in the fields alongside the men, gleaning and winnowing wheat, and hand pulling flax. It was hard, hot labor and the scenes show long lines of heavily laden female as well as male basket bearers carrying produce from field to storehouse. Women and men worked side by side at jobs indoors as well: grinding grain, brewing beer and baking bread. Tomb wall paintings show that both female and male servants waited on guests at banquets to which both women and men were invited. Women guests were not segregated off in their own quarters, but intermingled with the male guests at social as well as public events. There are several references in texts, both from the working class environment and the royal court, which describe men and women drinking together, they also participated together in funerals and other religious ceremonies.

Outside the home, even some non-elite women could exercise power and influence within their communities in impressive ways. At the community of royal artisans known today from the site of Deir el-Medina, the revered oracle of the deified queen Aḥmose-Nefertari would probably have needed a woman's voice. The "wise woman" or "divining woman" is a well-known figure in traditional societies even today, and she is mentioned in New Kingdom texts as well (Borghouts, 1994, 129-30; Wente, 1990, 141). How influential was she? Hers was a non-official power, but she was held in awe by her contemporaries. Posssibly every community had at least one such revered woman (a shaman) who could see beyond the obvious, predict the future, settle disputes, find lost property, advise the troubled and heal the sick. She was feared and respected and was a power in everyday life at the "grassroots" level of society, but she is barely visible to us now, unfortunately.

## The Home

While the sacred structures built by the Egyptians (whether temples or tombs) were meant to last for eternity and were thus built of stone, most of the dwellings of the people, be they princes or peasants, were built of mud brick. The remains of workers' towns show that the working class lived crowded together in small quarters. Houses were generally single story for the poor, with stairs to a roof top that might be used for sleeping, cooking and raising fowl. Workers' communities featured row houses and narrow alleys for streets, the whole surrounded by a wall for protection from marauding animals. Wealthier people in towns had two or three stories on their houses, or, if space permitted, spread out in a spacious single level that had adjacent granaries, workshops, and a pleasant pool surrounded by trees. An open loggia might front onto the garden.

Otherwise columns were used inside both simple and complex houses in order to raise the roofs of some rooms to utilize clerestory lighting. Windows were fitted with grates to emit only dim light, as temperature control was important in a land where summer temperatures are seldom comfortable. Whitewashed walls were decorated with paintings, often with themes of importance to the life and well-being of the women of the household. In the luxurious apartments of the palaces of Nefertiti and Ahkhenaten's new city, floors as well as walls were painted with lovely scenes of aquatic and bird life. Palaces and houses of the wealthy known from the New Kingdom were outfitted with dry toilets and stone-lined shower stalls fitted with drain pipes. Because the ceilings of tombs are painted with colorful intricate patterns, we assume that woven or appliquéed hangings were a feature of many homes as well. Furniture was simple and limited to basics: chairs and stools, small tables and beds. Clothing and other belongings were kept in lidded boxes on short legs or in commodious baskets.

The best known housing is that visible to any who visit Deir el-Medina, the ancient village site on the west bank at Luxor which was built by the government to house the skilled workmen employed to create the elaborate tombs of the royal family during the New Kingdom (Bierbrier, 1982; L. Lesko, 1994). Here, because it was so readily available, stone foundations were used for the row houses and thus their plans are well preserved. The rooms are arranged one behind the other and generally only number three or four, with an open air kitchen (for allowing smoke to escape) outfitted with brick ovens and with large stone mortars for the grinding of wheat. Off of this area were underground cellars for storage. While the second room was large and had brick divans for seating and a pottery hearth whose smoke could escape through the elevated roof, the first room of the house, open to the street, seems most associated with the Mistress of the Household. Here are often found high brick divans or "box-beds" approached by steps, which may have been designed as a quiet and safe corner for mothers with newborn infants (Friedman, 1994, 97-110). Walls adjacent to this structure were painted with images of the divinities of pregnancy and birth. Here too, in this first room of the house, the loom of the woman could well have been set up, as the most light would have been available from the open door and from here, too, a mother could keep an eye on her children and other passers-by in the street.

The average housewife of the above-mentioned civil-service community founded by the State was spared a lot of arduous labor (there was a laundry service staffed by men and time-shared slave women ground the wheat). The Mistress of the Household would have baked and cooked for her family, looked after small animals kept for food or hygiene (like pigs), and also maintained the cult of the ancestor and other religious rites important to her family's welfare (Friedman, 1994, 116). Families tended to be large, with preserved records showing eight or more living children, so most women were frequently pregnant and lost many babies to childhood illnesses.

Portrait of Nefertiti, painted limestone from Tell el-Amarna.    Courtesy of the Ägyptische Museum, Berlin.

Queen Nefertari-Merymut from her tomb in the Valley of the Queens.     Photo by David B. Larkin

Women mourners gathered at a funeral.  Tomb of Ramose, vizier of Amenhotep III.  Theban tomb no. 55.  Photo by L. H. Lesko

Woman offering milk.  Scene from tomb of Nakht, Theban Tomb No. 52.    Photo by B. S. Lesko

Temple of Amun at Karnak, viewed from across its sacred lake.    Photo by L. H. Lesko

Musicians entertaining at a banquet.  Tomb of Nakht, No. 52 at Thebes, Eithteenth Dynasty.     Photo by L. H. Lesko

Painting of the deified queen Ahmose-Nefertari and other deceased pharaohs (her son Amenhotep I is furthest to left).
Photo by L. H. Lesko.

Fashionably dressed couple listening to a harpist's song. Ramesside tomb of Inherkha, Deir el-Medina, no. 359.

Photo by L. H. Lesko.

Woman chantress from Thebes, holding up her *menit*-necklace. Tomb of Sennefer, No. 96. Photo by L. H. Lesko

Affectionate couple: Pairi and his wife Henut-nefert with their son Ptahmosi. Time of Amenhotep III. Theban tomb No. 139. Photo by L. H. Lesko.

Egyptian family of the New Kingdom fowling in the marshes. Theban tomb fragment, BM 37977.

Courtesy of the British Museum

# Women in the cults

Many women's lives were expanded beyond the confines of their home by their active participation in religious life and temple service. Religion was an important focus of Egyptian life at all class levels, ancestor cults were maintained by the women of the household who also kept shrines in their homes to divinities especially caring of women--the goddess Taweret portrayed as a pregnant hippo, and the bandy-legged lion headed dwarf Bes. Both of these helped women in pregnancy and childbirth and guarded the new born child.

Attendance on the deities in their numerous temples and shrines throughout the country was a role which appealed to many women, as well as men. A monument in New York's Metropolitan Museum of Art (09.180.18) reveals that already in the Old Kingdom is encountered a Chantress of Upper Egypt who participated and addressed the king directly in the very important national celebration of his *heb sed* or jubilee. Both male and female ka-servants looked after the mortuary cults of the deceased elite, pouring libations, making offerings and reciting the proper forumulas during these procedures (Blackman, 1921, 26). Also appearing in the Old Kingdom were entire troops of female temple musicians called *hener*, first only associated with goddess cults but later with funerals and with the cults of gods as well (Nord, 1981). There were female overseers of the *hener*, but, as the Old Kingdom progressed male participants are found as well, but the leadership positions were retained by women. Starting in the Old Kingdom *heners* performed at funerals, possibly because Hathor was viewed as the kindly deity of the West, who welcomed the deceased into the Beyond. Bare-breasted women dressed in short kilts danced while more fully clothed women clapped accompaniment and sang before the tomb's entrance. It may be that cultic celebrations of a sexual nature would have helped the dead be reborn again in the next world.

## Female Prophets

As early as the Old Kingdom, hundreds of non-royal women are known to have served as priests (*hm.t-ntr*) in the cults of important goddesses like Hathor and Neith. Although it is likely that social or economic status effected a woman's opportunities to belong in such exalted company, there was no sex discrimination with regard to holding the title of Prophet of Hathor. In fact, originally the priesthood of Hathor was predominantly female (Galvin, 1989, 29). Research on Old Kingdom Hathor cults has shown that a woman could be a

Old Kingdom limestone statue of a *mitr.t*-priestess. Photo courtesy of the P. A. Hearst Museum of Anthropology, University of California, Berkeley.

priestess in more than one temple, and that positions in the temple hierarchy were not inherited (Galvin, 1984). Thus the goddess's clergy were truly devout. While Galvin did not find examples of nepotism among them, she did find mother-in-law/daughter-in-law connections, probably indicating that older women in the cult tried to match-make to find a nice Hathor girl for their sons.

An Old Kingdom text reveals that a priestess with the rank of a *w'b.t* (pure one) received the same payment for her services as did a *w'b*-priest (Blackman, 1921, 25). Women with this title are found in the cult of Hathor and serving the gods Khons and Wepwawet (Blackman, 1921, 24-25). One *w'b.t*-woman was in charge of a royal weaving studio and mentions in a letter having to leave her job to serve her month of temple duty (Wente, 1990, 82). She obviously belonged to a phyle of a temple, to which she may have been initiated as a girl, as another Middle Kingdom letter mentions "the beautiful girl-children of the mortuary temple" of Senusert III jubilating for a ceremony (Wente, 1991, 77). Female *w'b.t*s are found as late as the Ptolemaic period in the cult of Amun in the Theban area.

Some priestesses of Hathor bore the title of *Mrt* which is a title for women attested from earliest times and throughout most of the Old Kingdom period (Blackman, 1921, 8). Their duty was to sing and play music to greet the king and the deity at the temple, but some *Mrt* priestesses appear to have been specifically charged with managing the fields and estates of the goddess. Thus these women held important responsibilities for real estate and agricultural personnel and ultimately for the financial security of their cult centers.

As the years went by, more men were attracted to the very popular and wide spread cult of Hathor, the most important goddess, but men usually left the priestly posts to women and filled a new position of Overseer of Priests, which hints at administrative responsibilities. As the temples had land, tenant farmers and other wealth, and as few women were literate, this may have been merely a practical recognition by the female clergy that they needed professionally trained men to help administer the endowments of some of the most important temples of the land, or it may indicate that men were determined to control the wealth of the temples and wrested this away from women.

Just how much prestige (and probably wealth) went along with the prophetship of the Hathor cult is indicated by the records of the Middle Egyptian province of Kusae where three generations of one elite family were leaders of the local Hathoric temple, with the governor being an overseer of priests and the women of his family being priestesses. The importance of the cult of Hathor is emphasized by the fact that the wives of kings generally were her priestesses in the state cult.

On the west bank at Luxor (ancient Thebes), there is a tomb of a lady of the Middle Kingdom who claimed the tomb, originally built by her husband, all for her own (Davies, 1920). She was married to a highly placed male official who chose, himself, to be buried in the north near his sovereign, Senusert II, whom he served as vizier (prime-minister). The lady Senet, thus, may have regarded herself as being divorced.  She removed from her side her husband's figure in the wall scenes and erased most of his titles and his name where they occurred, even though he was actually the most powerful man in Egypt next to the king. All three false door monuments in the tomb belong only to her, and thus she claimed the entire tomb for herself.  Senet had a large, over life-sized and beautifully sculpted statue created for her funerary cult and tells us that she was an honored lady and priestess of Hathor, honored by Hathor in the midst of the necropolis.  It is obvious that she could pass into the other world in her own right, and actually this is just what the Coffin Texts, the mortuary literature of the time ensured. The funerary literature that once was reserved for royalty had become, around the end of the third millennium B.C., the First Intermediate Period, taken up by commoners.  Those who could afford a coffin would now have these magical texts written on its boards.

Later in the Middle Kingdom the large tombs of provincial elite disappear and testimonies to women in the cults at high levels appear less frequently (Gillam, 1995). However, a priestess of Hathor's cult in the Sinai is attested as late as the reign of Amenemhet III, so it is dangerous to jump to conclusions on the non-existence of data and even men have not left many monuments from this period that can elucidate clearly the priestly hierarchies. In the early New Kingdom we once again find both men and women active in Hathor's cult, some of each sex with titles indicating positions as entertainers (Davies and Gardiner, 1915, pls. 19 & 20). From later in the New Kingdom, comes documentation indicating the wife of a male high priest of Hathor was the leader of the entertainers (the *ḥener*) of the temple (Kitchen, 1978, 286, 301-302).  As in the case of all major deities during the New Kingdom, the professionalization of the priesthood had positioned men at the top of the hierarchy, but wives and daughters are invariably found also playing major roles in the same temple.  The depictions of Queen Nefertari sacrificing before various gods in her tomb and temple suggests that she and probably other royal women also still had primary functions in the cults of leading deities.  This corresponds with titles used by a princess of that family.

## The God's Wives and Divine Adoratrices

In the Old Kingdom, women served as prophets, not only for the cults of goddesses, but in the cults of male deities like Thoth, and Ptah (Fischer, 1982, 1101).  One of the highest ranks a woman could attain in a cult of a god was the singular position known as the God's Wife. In the Middle Kingdom at least two women with this title are found: one serving the cult of Min the fertility god of Akhmim and the other Amun of Thebes, who would become, in the New Kingdom, head of the entire pantheon as Amun-Re, king of the gods. During the New Kingdom, the title of God's Wife of Amun was held by royal women, first by Queen Aḥhotep and then Aḥmose Nefertari, next attested with Hatshepsut and her daughter Neferure, and later with the mothers of Amenhotep II and Thutmose IV (Robins, 1993, 150).  When the Amun cult was abandoned by

Lady of the House, Mutemuia, holding up her sistrum.  Theban tomb 178, reign of Ramses II.

Akhenaten and Nefertiti this position too disappeared, although royal women are shown officiating in the new state cult. Later the position of God's Wife of Amun was resurrected, held by the queens of the Nineteenth Dynasty.

Another high female temple rank was Divine Adoratrice, which in the Eighteenth Dynasty was sometimes held by women of high status at court (like the mother-in-law of a king) or by the wife of the high priest (First Prophet) in the Amun cult at Karnak. Under Queen Hatshepsut we meet in this capacity one Sensoneb, the daughter of the First Prophet, married to the Second Prophet. In the tomb she shared with her husband the couple is portrayed as inspecting estates and receiving produce, which may indicate the estates belonged to the temple they served (Whale, 1989, 52). The increase of women's visibility in the monuments of the Eighteenth dynasty (following a long period of seemingly lessened involvement after the Old Kingdom) has been attributed to the presence of a female on the throne of the pharaohs (Whale, 1989, 241, 275) as have the increase in women's cult titles (Bryan, 1984, 15).

Frequently in the late New Kingdom's tomb paintings and on stelae women are shown confronting the deity directly, making offerings to it or performing rites for deceased family members. Thus women may have played a more vital role in their religion than often credited them. They do not seem to have been relegated to being merely musical accompanists in religious ceremonies.

Stela of offering to an ancestor bust. Reproduced from Florence Friedman's chapter in *Pharaoh's Workers,* ed. by L. H. Lesko, Cornell University Press, 1994. Used by permission of the publisher.

Several late Ramesside letters reveal that women participated in the administration of temples. For instance, one Chantress of Amon-Re named Henuttowy has left a long letter addressed to her husband, the necropolis scribe Nesamenope, describing how she received grain shipments for the temple she served and was responsible for getting food offerings to the altar (Wente, 1990, 174-5). Another woman, a Principal of the *Hener* of Amon Re, named Herere, was in the position of ordering a troop captain to distribute pay rations to the royal necropolis workers (Wente, 1990, 200-1).

The priesthood, which now held its titles and wealth at the pleasure of pharaoh, saw itself as a select and prestigious group and its families attempted to hold posts for generations. Thus we find, in Nineteenth Dynasty records, marriages uniting different priestly families of high rank (Bierbrier, 1975). The wives of the chief prophets tended to be superiors of the *hener* of the temple. Private monuments of the elite classes of the New Kingdom are replete with the titles of women who served as either chantresses or singers in at least one, and often several, temple cults and thus were members of their *hener*. Most of these women also use the title Lady of the House and most were probably married. However, the prestige of their cultic associations was such that husbands would address letters to them using the lady's cultic title (Wente, 1990, 162; 174). Not all women with important religious affiliations were necessarily married, however. There is a record, from the Twentieth Dynasty (Peet, 1930, 39), of at least four tombs belonging to the chantresses of the House of the Divine Votaress of Amun-Re, King of the Gods, suggesting that some women attracted to the religious life remained single and consecrated exclusively to the preeminent god.

After Egypt's empire faded and the country became divided into separate political camps, the virtual ruler of Upper Egypt was the high priest of Karnak, who married a royal princess to increase his power. Daughters of the High Priest then filled the role of God's Wife of Amun but also took the old queenly title of Lady of the Two Lands and wrote their names inside the royal cartouche. Other women of the family served as Prophetess of Mut, the goddess who was Amun's consort (Naguib, 1988, 287; Kitchen, 1973, 275-86). Whether this office had always been filled by women is not known, although an oracle of Mut is mentioned in a New Kingdom text and one would expect it would have had a female voice.

## Female Pontiffs

By the Twenty-Third Dynasty, Egypt was under Libyan rule and the fourth king of that dynasty, Osorkon III (777-749 B.C.) consecrated his own daughter as a celibate God's Wife who would live in Thebes and give all her attention to the god's cult (Kitchen, 1973, 359). This priestess was Shepenwepet I who received all the estates and property formerly possessed by the High Priest. She ensured her succession by adopting a successor, and this younger woman carried the old title of Divine Adoratrice. As these women enjoyed long lives that spanned kingly reigns, they were a source of moral and political stability and leadership. As they were dedicated to Amun and looked after Karnak and the rest of his domain (the entire Thebaid), they may have won credibility and the loyalty of the Upper Egyptians far more readily than could have any military prince in the high priest position. Egyptologists generally credit the God's Wives with being the true leaders of Upper Egypt, with great spiritual and temporal power. However just how much independence they had is difficult to judge. One emminent scholar has written recently that the Divine Adoratrice at Thebes "was the only person capable of defusing the latent conflict" between Saites and Kushites, the two predominant political camps in this Late Period (Grimal, 1992, 365). At least in religious matters this woman was very like a female pope and would have ruled by the word of Amun, probably by manipulating his oracle.

When the Nubians invaded to wrest Egypt away from the Libyans, these southern people were also devoted to the god Amun. Thus a princess of their royal house was inserted into the line of succession at Thebes. The first Nubian God's Wife was Amenirdis, the sister of the general Piay, who returned to the southern kingdom of Kush leaving his sister in Egypt as his representative (Kitchen, 1973, 237-9). She in turn adopted as her successor Piay's daughter to be known as Shepenwepet II. Her reign saw the invasion by the Assyrians and the sack of Thebes. Karnak temple was robbed of its treasure (including solid gold obelisks) but Shepenwepet managed to survive. Pyloned funerary chapels for her and her successors were built within the confines of the great mortuary temple of Ramses III at Medinet Habu on the west bank of Thebes. However, Shepenwepet was forced, before she died, to adopt as her successor the princess of a new royal house, the Twenty-Sixth Dynasty.

The adoption of the princess Nitocris was recorded on a great granite stela at Karnak which tells how she was escorted from the Delta to Thebes in a long procession of boats bearing much dowry (Caminos, 1964; Kitchen, 1973, 403). Her immense wealth was administered for her by a major-domo (Nitocris had four during her reign) appointed by her father. It is clear that king Psammetichus I intended to control the expenditures on major projects in Thebes and that the major-domo would answer to him. However, once her father died, Nitocris appointed her own men who were loyal to her: men of Thebes rather than men of the Delta. This independent woman reigned on for over 50 years without even adopting a successor and that way kept the kings from having influence in the South. Finally, in 594 B.C. and in her eighties, Nitocris adopted her great niece Ankhnesneferibre, daughter of Psammetichus II, soon after he came to the throne of Egypt.

This young woman was given the title of First Prophet or High Priest of Amun. Ankhnesneferibre is the only woman known to have held this high clerical office. Clearly Nitocris, who must have engineered this move, was determined to preserve the importance of women at Karnak. During the 130 years of these two women's reigns, their power definitely rivaled the kings of their time, certainly in Upper Egypt. Ankhnesneferibre's beautiful stone sarcophagus shows her effigy wearing an age-old queen's headdress and holding the crook and flail scepters of Egypt.

Relief of Shepenwepet from her tomb chapel

The tomb chapels of Amenirdis and Shepenwepet at Medinet Habu

## Excerpts from Love Poems

### Chester Beatty I, verso, C3, 110-4,6

As I was passing by
    In the neighborhood of his house
I found its door open and
    my lover standing beside his mother
    and all his brethren.
Admiration of him seized the heart
    of all who walked along the road...
Perfect boy without equal!
    a lover choice of character!
He noticed me when I passed by,
    but I must rejoice privately.
How delighted is my heart with pleasure!
    Since (you) behold me!
Would that my mother knew my wish,
    she would go inside for a time.
Golden One, please put it in her mind,
    then I shall hasten to my lover,
    and kiss him in front of his companions.
I would not be embarrassed because of the (other)
    people.
I would be happy because of their realization that
    you know me,
    and I would make feasts for my goddess.
My heart is impatient to go forth,
    in order that I might gaze upon my lover in the
    night.
How wonderful is this passing by!

### Papyrus Chester Beatty I, recto 7, 3

I've drawn near you to see your love,
O prince of my heart!
How lovely is my hour (with you)
(this) hour flows forth for me forever---
It began when I lay with you.
In sorrow and in joy,
You have exalted my heart.
Do not (leave) me.

### Cairo Ostracon 25218

The lover of the lady is here while she is on yonder
    shore.
The river is around my limbs.
The flood is mighty in its season.
The crocodile lurks upon the shoal,
    While I descend further into the waters
    In order to submit myself to the current.
My heart is confident upon the channel.
I found the aforementioned (crocodile) like a mouse,
    And the waters like land unto my feet,
It is her love that causes me to be (so) strong.

Men and women guests at a
banquet.  Fragment of a Theban
tomb scene, B.M. 37986
   Courtesy of the British Museum

# Sex, marriage and family life

Egypt of antiquity celebrated its women. Few of the world's cultures have created such favorable female images. Egyptian art portrayed the average woman--even of the servant class--as slim, attractive and dignified. On the other hand, the female figure was nearly always emphasized by the traditional portrayal of unrealistically skin-tight dresses, even though actual dresses could not have been so clinging. This is true even for elite women, but not the case with the portrayals of elite men whose bodies are often quite enveloped by robes. It is likely that the artistic canon was expressing, with such very physical depictions of all women, the sexual role of the female as the "fertile field" essential for the perpetuation of the family expressed by the sage Ptahhotep in the earliest wisdom literature.

While the married woman must have attained a special importance when she bore children and assumed the great responsibilities of feeding and clothing her family, the Egyptian woman's independent status, underwritten by the law, was reflected in the freedom with which she conducted her personal life. The preceding poems and many others are examples of the love songs which tell of sensual love between unmarried lovers. The majority of the songs are presented as the words of women. Young men and women seem to have socialized together before marriage. There was no word for virginity in the ancient Egyptian vocabulary, and apparently sexual liaisons were permitted before marriage for both sexes. Once marriage was entered into, however, both husband and wife were expected to remain loyal.

By the New Kingdom, it was quite normal for a wife and husband to refer to one another endearingly as "sister" and "brother" though no blood relationship existed. Some poignant testimonials of the love and consideration which wives received are contained in letters which bereaved and troubled husbands wrote to their deceased wives and left at their tombs:

> "Now when I went accompanying Pharaoh, l[ife]. p[rosperity]. h[ealth]., in journeying south this condition (death) befell you, and I spent these several months without eating or drinking like a normal person. When I arrived in Memphis, I begged leave of Pharaoh, l.p.h., and [came] to where you were. And I and my people wept sorely for you before [you] (i.e. your body) in my quarter (?). I donated clothing of fine linen to wrap you up and had many clothes made. I overlooked nothing good so as not to have it done for you. Now look, I've spent these last three years without entering (another) house although it is not proper that one who is in the same situation as I be made to do this. Now look, I've done this out of consideration for you." (Wente, 1990, 217).

Egypt's New Kingdom, with its foreign empire and wealth, saw the development of a class of knights, wealthy and literate charioteers who accompanied pharaoh into battle as an elite company. When they pursued the arts of peace, these gentlemen, like their counterparts in the later European Middle Ages, discovered love to be eternal and idyllic, and an inspiration for poetry. In this courtly love poetry, the lady love is idealized, compared to goddesses, inspires feats of strength and daring, or is the cause of prolonged love sickness and the abject submission of her lover (B. Lesko, 1986, 95). The empire of the Eighteenth dynasty spawned an effete culture which adopted elaborate fashions and affected foreign habits. Judging from the artistic renditions of women, which show them more ornamented, buxom, and glamorous in large curled wigs, ladies of high society now seem more valued (at least by the artists) for their appearance than for their character or capabilities.

Biblical accounts of the licentiousness of the Egyptians and Canaanites are probably sheer hyperbole written to cast the Enemy in a bad light (e.g. Leviticus 18). The art of pharaonic Egypt certainly veered away from the obscene. The one papyrus surviving from pharaonic times with drawings depicting heterosexual couples engaged in sex portrays no "unnatural" acts and is more playful than pornographic. Homosexuality was condemned, judging from the lists of "sins" to be denied by any wishing safe passage into the realm of Osiris on the day of judgment. On the other hand, incest may have been practiced by some royal families who saw themselves as divinities, not to be held to the same standards as their human subjects (Middleton, 1962). The gods, after all, did indulge in sexual alliances between siblings and fathers and daughters.

Nudity or scanty dress came quite naturally to the inhabitants of this semi-arid land. The poorer the person, the less clothing he or she apparently wore. Servant women often shown as working stripped to the waist, and informal sketches on ostraca of housewives found at the village site of Deir el Medina suggest that near nudity was not unusual in everyday life. Full dress may have been for important occasions, although seasonal temperatures would have demanded more clothing in winter. Royal women donned linen so fine as to be transparent and even though worn in layers would have allowed glimpses of bare limbs. Thus prudery was not a factor among the Egyptians, as exemplified by the numerous votives in the shape of phalli and vulvae left at holy shrines by the faithful who prayed earnestly for fertility and the possibility of offspring (Pinch, 1993, pl. 52).

### Marriages

In theory, an Egyptian woman might marry whomever she pleased, but what was possible was not necessarily always practiced, as elite families at least would have probably arranged marriages, just as royalty did. As we saw with the cult of Hathor, a number of mother-in-law and daughter-in-law associations prevailed which suggest that older women in temple service found wives for their sons from among the young acquaintances they made at the temple. The genealogies of the high clergy (which extend over a surprisingly long series of generations) show much intermarriage with other high priestly families (Bierbrier, 1975; Kitchen, 1973).

The love poems of the New Kingdom speak of a young man appealing to a mother for her daughter's hand, but actual non-literary documents show that the father of the family viewed himself as his daughter's protector and sought guarantees on her behalf that both financial and physical security would be forthcoming for her. One father of a bride demanded that the prospective son-in-law take an oath promising to submit himself to 100 lashes if he ever mistreated his wife (Ward, 1963, 431). Another father wrote to his daughter: "You are my good daughter. If the worker Baki throws you out of the house, I will take action..."(Wente, 1990, 147). The great disparity between the ages of wife and husband, so common in patriarachal societies, does not seem to have been popular among the Egyptians whose sages urged men to marry young. Marriage among the commoners was overwhelmingly monogamous and legitimate marriage had to be a union between equals and between free people. It could not take place between a free person and a slave without the slave (male or female) first being freed and given some property.

Women at a banquet. Scene from tomb of Nakht, Theban Tomb 52

As heirs were of major importance--promising security in old age and ensuring immortality after death--a barren wife risked divorce, although some couples simply adopted an heir or resorted to a slave woman as a surrogate mother without harming the status of the first wife as Mistress of the House. In antiquity many wives predeceased their husbands due to the hazards of pregnancy, and thus funerary monuments can show a man with more than one wife even if they were successive. The Egyptians had a word for "second wife" denoting, not polygamy, but the fact that many a man outlived his first wife and would have another before he died. The wealthy farmer Ḥeḳanakhte who lived in the Eleventh Dynasty and left a packet of letters behind, which somehow managed to survive almost 4000 years, was quite upset that the sons of his first marriage were giving his new wife a hard time (James, 1962).

Usually the state took no interest in recording marriages and, as far as now known, no religious ceremony consecrated a wedding. It was simply a social action, accompanied by feasting and gift giving between the parties involved. The groom gave a gift to the bride's parents, and made a declaration of his wealth and ability to support a wife decently. From the late Twentieth Dynasty survives a marriage document that was preceded by a session in the vizier's court. A man who had a grown family with his first wife was intent on protecting the wife of his second marriage by having his children declare satisfaction with the inheritance that already had been granted them. Thus the second wife was given a large share in property of her husband that included slaves. This would be shared by the couple during their marriage and would come to the wife in the event of the husband dying or divorcing her, unless the divorce was for adultery on her part, in which case she forfeited her right to her marriage settlement (Černý & Peet, 1927, 37). During the Late Period (9th to the 6th Century B.C.) marriage documents occur in which a bride groom dealt with the father of the bride, pledging his property to him as security for the "gift for the woman" (Johnson, 1994, 114). Later documents show a change, with the woman becoming a more active partner in the agreement (Allam, 1985, 36).

How much freedom of movement Egyptian women enjoyed is indicated by one New Kingdom pharaoh boasting of his maintaining such order in the realm that women could travel along the public highway unmolested. However rape of an enemy's wife was threatened in curses, so women were victims in this society too. The fact that women were able to walk about in public unveiled and unchaperoned inspired sagely warnings to young men to beware of a strange woman from another town: "a deep water whose currents one knows not." This suggests that most people grew up and married and lived out their lives in the same community, and that the small, intermarried community enforced proper behavior among all its citizens. Indeed, the records from Deir el-Medina show that marriages within extended families occurred (for instance, cousins marrying cousins and sometimes uncles their nieces) and that brides were thus not "strangers" who were placed in vulnerable and uncomfortable positions socially when they married. However, there are also records of wives at ancient Thebes who had affiliations with cults of deities known from towns more than a day's journey away. This suggests more mobility of the population, and at least some middle class marriages made outside the home community.

Marriage was regarded as the ideal state for adults, but perhaps was deemed more the right of those with some independence and wealth, as the Egyptian phrase for marriage was "to found a house." The urban family of the New Kingdom seems to have been nuclear, with the young couple living by themselves in their own house, but extended families were probably more commonly found in the countryside, where economic necessity would keep farm acreage ideally within the hands of one family, all of whose members were needed for labor. Throughout ancient Egyptian history, women were able to own land, and the sage Ani speaks of a wife's house as "her house," and in court testimony one sometimes finds married women referring to their own house. In one case a couple must have been residing with the wife's father as the elder forbids his son-in-law access to their home as long as he is suspected of tomb robbing.

No matter how it was arranged initially, the existence of bonds of love between husbands and wives is well documented. Affection and consideration for the women of the family can be seen as one of the most common motifs of tomb art, where the wife is always present (and successive wives are too if the first died young). In both the Old Kingdom and New Kingdom sculpture and wall scenes, portrayals of husbands and wives with arms around each other or holding hands were quite common. A wife's name in a family tomb or other monument is often prefixed with the affectionate: "his beloved." Because most tombs of the Old Kingdom were not built by the family that used them, but were gifts from the king to the husband who served him as an official or courtier, the royal artisans who created the tomb concentrated on portraying the courtier and gave much less attention to members of his family. Thus there are virtually no autobiographical texts concerning women of the family, but there are a few epitaphs which include "revered with her husband" and "whom people praise." Highly placed women, like priestesses and members of the royal family, had tombs of their own in the Old Kingdom.

Consideration towards women was sanctioned by society. The Vizier Ptahhotep of the Old Kingdom is credited with this advice to his son:

> *"If you are well-to-do and establish a household, love your wife with passion. Fill her belly, clothe her back, oil is a prescription of her body. Cause her to be happy all the time you exist. She is a profitable field for her lord."*

The sage added that a woman's intelligence should not be under-rated when he observed that "fine speech is more hidden than green stone, but it is found with servant women at the millstones."

While attributed to a sage of the Old Kingdom, Ptahhotep, these sayings probably originated in the feudal Middle Kingdom and reflect the sentiments of that time, rather than the earlier period in which women seem to have taken an even more active role in society. The instructions reflect a patriarchal stance, viewing a husband as a wife's "lord." Later, an equally widely read sage of the New Kingdom named Ani held more liberal views:

> *"You should not be over-bearing with a woman in her house when you know that she if efficient. Do not say to her "where is it, fetch it for us," Let your eye be watchful while you are silent that you might perceive her skillfulness. Happiness is when your hand is together with hers."*

He preached fidelity in marriage too:

> *"Every man who marries should keep firm the rapid heart. Do not go off after a woman; do not let her steal your heart."*

These examples from Egyptian "wisdom literature" presented as advice from wise men to their sons, actually circulated and were read more widely. Nowhere in them do we find any admonition to teach wives respect and obedience, nor do we find recommendations to beat wives or otherwise chastise them. Women were not perceived as inferiors, and the student is taught to respect the women of the household, family and servants alike. Reflecting this, men of the Old Kingdom would state in their tomb inscriptions: "I was respectful to my father and gracious to my mother." Correspondents in the New Kingdom even used formal address in letters to their wives and mothers including the religious title of the lady if she had one.

There is also this remarkable reminiscence in a letter from a husband to his wife: "When I was instructing officers for Pharaoh's infantry and his chariotry, I [had[ them come and prostrate themselves before you, bringing every sort of fine thing to set before [you]" (Wente, 1990, 217). Respect for one's social superiors was expected to be demonstrated and thus social rank sometimes is of more importance than gender in determining status, although it can be argued that the lady in question was probably honored because of her husband's importance. As Ani commented: "a man is asked about his rank, a woman about her husband's."

## The Family

One New Kingdom Egyptian woman is on record as commenting in public "What is the God of a person except his father and his mother?" From an earlier period, a man advised: "Praise god for your father and your mother who set you on the path of life." Thus both parents are credited with the socialization of their children, but in actual fact many men list only the mother as parent in their inscriptions, and this is true even among the elite. Esteem for her is obvious in the tomb art and the inscriptions of all periods, and in the wisdom literature. Mothers of grown and married sons are often portrayed on family monuments. Sometimes mothers are placed in the most conspicuous place of honor, as in the Twelfth Dynasty stelae, overshadowing the wife in importance. Many more stelae (inscribed tablets) survive as private monuments than any other form, and because these could accommodate several figures, whole families including servants were often portrayed. In the Middle Kingdom, before deities were portrayed on private monuments, it was usual to place together the figures of the entire family, father, mother and children in the top register or in the top two registers. A man's mother sometimes replaces his wife in the closest positioning to his figure on the stela, but often all are accommodated, with the mother facing the son and his family. The father of the stela dedicator is sometimes given a less important position and will not even be named, although the mother of the owner will be named (Pfluger, 1947).

The large rock hewn tomb sculptures of the New Kingdom family will often show husband mother and wife. Sometimes the Eighteenth Dynasty wife is depicted in the wall scenes making an offering to her mother-in-law, suggesting that, as in the royal family, a man's mother could be the most important woman in his family. Obviously the many arduous duties and skills required to feed and clothe an ancient family were passed on from mothers to daughters, but mothers are credited with rearing their sons too. The New Kingdom sage Any urged his readers to honor their mothers for the patient and devoted care and the years of education they had provided their sons.

> *Double the food your mother gave you.*
> *Support her as she supported you*
> *She had a heavy load in you,*
> *But she did not abandon you.*
> *When you were born after your months,*
> *She was yet yoked (to you),*
> *Her breast in your mouth for three years.*
> *As you grew and your excrement disgusted,*
> *She was not disgusted, saying: "What shall I do!"*
> *When she sent you to school,*
> *and you were taught to write,*
> *She kept watching over you daily,*
> *With bread and beer in her house*
> The Maxims of Any, ( Lichtheim, 1976, 141)

Motherhood was acknowledged in the decoration of house interiors as well. Excavated houses reveal wall paintings in main rooms which celebrated the birth and suckling of babies (Kemp, 1979; Friedman, 1994, 100). Indeed the process of parturition and post-parturition seems to have been an occasion of much festivity. The bed of the mother, traditionally decorated with garlands of leaves for the occasion of her confinement, may be the permanent divan found in the front room of some workers' houses. It could also, of course, have been the safest place to keep a very young baby away from the dirt, vermin, and animals on the floor of most humble houses. At any rate, the walls were painted with dadoes of the protective genius Bes, whose amulet, for its magical powers, would also have been attached to the child. The woman in labor had the help and support of friends and family, religious amulets and deities such as the perpetually pregnant hippopotamus goddess Taweret.

Contrary to popular opinion about antiquity, it was not unusual for upper class people with sedentary life-styles, like priests and scribes, to live into their seventies and eighties. Some kings are known to have lived even longer. It is women who brought down the average life expectancy, as so many died in childbirth. Thus many men had at least two wives during their lifetimes. Having an heir, who would, not only help support them in old age but see to the proper burial of the parents and the maintenance of mortuary services, was extremely important to Egyptians. In order to ensure them the enjoyment of eternal life, the names of deceased persons could not be allowed to be forgotten. The reciting of prayers on the deceased's behalf, the leaving of food and drink at the tomb, and the preservation of a monument whose inscription would ask for such benefices throughout eternity, were duties that the living could fulfill on behalf of their parents and ancestors. This is one of the reasons the sage Any urged his students to marry while still young and to produce heirs:

> *It is proper to make people*
> *Happy the man whose people are many*

Children, both daughters and sons, were beloved by the Egyptians. Classical authors remarked that the Egyptians raised all of their children and did not engage in infanticide. Those who had no progeny frequently resorted to adoption, and a successful man who had no son might take on as both an apprentice and a surrogate son a young man of promise. It was said that everyone needed an eldest son who would "pour water on the hands" of his parents. Tomb scenes usually show the eldest son officiating at the burial of one or the other of his parents and at their memorial, although sometimes, in lieu of a brother, a daughter did this for her parents.

Widows in the ancient Near East pursued a more independent life than most married women, providing they had some property (Kuhrt, 1989, 226). One widow of the Twentieth Dynasty was pursued by a man who twice proposed marriage (or the wish to share her domicile), but each time she rebuffed him. However, the lot of the widow was often hard, as she and the orphan are named for special charity by leading male citizens who wish to be remembered on their monuments as being magnanimous. The later sage Amenemopet instructed:

> "*Do not take notice of a widow when*
> *you catch her (gleaning) in the fields*
> *and do not fail to indulge her response...*
> *God has desired the feeding of the poor*
> *more than the honoring of the wealthy.*"

Without a male protector, or an extended family network, both women and children might have to sell themselves as indentured servants or worse. Their fates would be greatly influenced by their skills, their social contacts, and their family wealth.

## Family wealth and inheritance

Marriage documents, surviving from the end of the New Kingdom and later, were drawn up once the married couple had children. This demonstrates that the right of the children to inherit from their parents was being protected. Property acquired by the married couple during their marriage became joint property. The husband had the right of usufruct, that is the right to invest or dispose of this wealth, but had to make restitution to his wife of her share whenever she might demand it, as in a divorce case. If the deed to a house was kept in the wife's name (as when she might have inherited from her parents) she alone had the right to dispose of the property

Surviving from the Late Period are "annuity contracts" made by a man on behalf of a female relative (wife, daughter or daughter-in-law) which guaranteed her an annual maintaince with the male's property as security for this arrangement. In one known case, the woman kept and passed on this "annuity" even upon her divorce from the man's son (Johnson, 1994, 124). Because they inherited wealth and were legally independent persons, women were able to enter into legal contracts on their own and surviving documents show they purchased slaves and property and made loans (Pestman, 1981, 295-315).

In the case of a husband's death, his wife received one-third of the joint estate plus her own property, and their children were entitled to divide the remaining two-thirds of the parents' joint estate and stood to inherit their mother's when she died. If the wife died first, her children were entitled to her one-third and whatever she had inherited from her parents (Johnson, 1996).

If a man divorced his wife, he had to return any dowry she may have brought into the marriage and pay her a fine, unless he could prove adultery as the basis of the divorce (Allam, 1989). A wife could initiate a divorce, but doubtless had difficulty in obtaining further support from her ex-husband, although some texts (including the above-mentioned "annuity texts") indicate she had a legal right to support. Once divorced, both partners had the right to remarry. Divorce is known to have followed adulterous affairs, although the stories and wisdom texts relate that death at the hands of the injured husband might well be the fate of one or both of the parties in the affair.

The welfare of a second wife could be secured by the legal fiction of adopting her as one of her husband's children. In a known case, the children of his first marriage swore not to contest this arrangement (Gardiner, 1940). They had already inherited from their mother and a portion of their father's estate was assured them, but now more recently acquired wealth would be entailed for the second wife.

In one Old Kingdom case a man credited his wealth to his mother, even though his father was still living (Fischer, 1989, 9). The Middle Kingdom's records show the right to the governance of provinces, in that feudal age, could pass through the women of the family, a young man inheriting his uncle's position from his mother for instance. Marriage documents and other legal texts from the New Kingdom show that, upon marriage a daughter of wealthy parents was given houses, land and retainers, and this constituted most of what she stood to inherit from their estate. But her young husband would not inherit from his parents until their death. Thus in some families, the wife had more economic independence than her husband, who presumably had to stay on good terms with his elders and be prepared to bury them in order to become their heir. In many cases parental estates were split among siblings, although, if one child assumed the entire responsibility of burying his parents, it was commonly considered his right to inherit the largest share of their property. Of course there are instances of daughters having to assume this responsibility too, and it was regarded as the duty of children to look after their parents in their last years. In one documented case a daughter is sued in court by her mother for neglect, and in another case a mother disinherited four of her eight children for not looking after her as well as they might have (even though her husband was still living) (Černý, 1945).

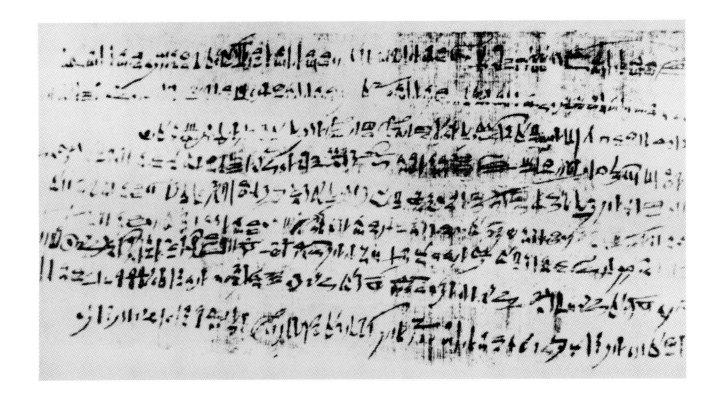

A page from the will of the Lady Naunakht. Permission to reproduce from the *Journal of Egyptian Archaeology* 31, courtesy of the Egypt Exploration Society, London

In summary, it is obvious that ancient Egyptian women led both public and private lives. They were certainly not hesitant to appear in public, whether as traders in the market place, as celebrants in sacred cults and funerals, or supporting their husbands in the first recorded labor strike in history (Edgerton, 1951, 137-40). The records of daily life are so sparse for much of Egypt's long history--so much information has been lost--that it is not possible to reconstruct all the details concerning women's participation in ancient Egyptian society. Her roles certainly varied with her rank and with the times in which she lived. Once documentation survives in greater amounts, from the Late Period, it is clear that Egyptian women held "a wide range of rights" and "owned a significant amount of private property" (Allam, 1990, 32). Most likely she was even earlier more involved in the public sphere than generally acknowledged. We long for the stories behind such epithets as this from the Old Kingdom "whom all her town loved."

When we take the trouble to examine Egyptian records and make comparisons to other cultures of antiquity and more recent ages, the social condition of the ancient Egyptian woman is remarkable. Consider, for instance, the women of ancient Greece with their restricted lives, cloistered at home with children and distaff, while the men of that society filled the markets, theaters, stadia, and lawcourts. In that patrilineal society scholars taught young men that women were their inferiors in every respect, and Athenian husbands and wives were not even found together at social events like private dinner parties. Even in Egypt, the women of the immigrant Greek population, living under their own laws during the Ptolemaic dynasty, are found needing guardians in their legal transactions--even a son had authority over a mother in this public context.

In contrast the native Egyptian woman was an independent legal personality and the Egyptian couple went everywhere together, sharing life's trials and delights as respected and equal citizens in their secular and religious communities, enjoying equality under the law. While this was one of Egypt's glories, it was, unfortunately, not to be her legacy. It was classical culture which influenced later European society and, in time, our own.

# Selective Chronology of

## Ancient Egyptian History

Unification of the Two Lands of Upper and Lower Egypt into one nation, capital at Memphis. c. 3150 B.C.

### Old Kingdom

Third Dynasty -- first large scale construction in stone: 2660 B.C.
  Queen Nymaathap; Princess Hetephernebty associated with King Djoser.
Fourth Dynasty -- pyramids of Giza--2625-2510
  King Sneferu and Queen Hetepheres I
  Khufu (Cheops) and Queens Meritites and Henutsen
  Redjedef and Hetepheres II
  Khafre and Meresankh III and Khamerernebty I
  Menkaure and Khamerernebty II
  Shepseskaf and Bunefer
Fifth Dynasty -- pyramid texts, sun temples:
  King Userkaf and Queen Khentkawes 2510-2460
Sixth Dynasty -- the beginning of decentralized government;
  Pyramid texts for queens: Pepi I and queens Ankhesenmeryre I and II, latter regent for Pepi II; Queen
  Nitokerty, King of Upper and Lower Egypt.

### First Intermediate Period

Seventh Dynasty to Eighth Dynasty -- weak kings continue rule at Memphis.
Ninth and Tenth Dynasty -- ruling from Herakleopolis, great literary activity, including Coffin Texts.
Eleventh Dynasty--powerful provincial governors. 2160-2040

### Middle Kingdom
2040-1674

Twelfth Dynasty -- strong centralized government emerges again ruling from It-tawy, suburb of Memphis.
  King Amenemhet founds new royal family line.
  Senusert I and Queen Neferu
  Senuscrt II and Queen Khenemetneferhedjet Weret
  Senusert III and Queen Mereseger
    Queen Neferhent; Princess Sat-Hathor-Iunit
  Amenemhet III and Queen Hetepti
  Queen Sobekneferu (daughter of Amenemhet III) ruler.

### Second Intermediate Period
1674-1553

Thirteenth Dynasty -- ruling from Memphis
Fourteenth Dynasty -- ruling from Xois
Fifteenth and Sixteenth Dynasty (Hyksos) ruling from Avaris (Tell el-Dab'a).
Seventeenth Dynasty--ruling from Thebes
  King Senakhtenre Ta'o I and Tetisheri
  Sekenenre Ta'o and Ahhotep
  Kamose; Ahmose I

### New Kingdom
1552-1069

Eighteenth Dynasty--return to Memphis as capital; Foreign wars, imperialistic expansion.
  Ahmose I and Ahmose-Nefertari
  Amenhotep I and Ahhotep
  Thutmose I and Ahmose
  Thutmose II and Hatshepsut

Hatshepsut  1490-1469
Thutmose III and Merytre-Hatshepsut
Amenhotep II and Ti'o and Ahmose-
      Merytamon
Thutmose IV and Mutemwia and I'r.t
Amenhotep III and Tiy  1390-1352
Akhenaton and Nefertiti
Smenkhkare and Merytaton
Tutankahamun and Ankhesenamun
Aye and Ti
Haremheb and Mutnodjme

Nineteenth Dynasty--ruling from Memphis and
      the Delta
Ramses I and Sitre
Seti I and Tuy
Ramses II  1279-1212 and Nefertari-
      Merymut, Esenofer, and Hittite
      Princess Maathorneferure. Meryt-
      amun, Bintanat,
      Nebettawy, Tanedjem and
      Isitnofret are daughters who were
      official wives as well.
Tauseret, monarch and regent for Siptah
      1196-1188.

Twentieth Dynasty
      Ramses III and Queens Isis and
         Habadilat

## Third Intermediate Period
(Post Empire)     1069-702

Twenty First Dynasty--ruling from Tanis
      Smendes and Queens Tentamun and
         Henuttawy
      Psusennes I and Mutnodjemet
      High Priests ruling at Thebes
         Piankh and Henuttawy
         Pinudjem I and Henuttawy II
         Pinudjem II and Istemkheb IV
         Osorkon and Maaatkare II
Twenty Second (Libyan) Dynasty
      The Shoshenq's and Osorkon's

*The God's Wives at Thebes*
      Karomama-Merytmut
Twenty-Third Dynasty
      Shepenwepet I
Piankhy from Kush
      Amenirdis I
      Shepenwepet II

## The Late Period

Twenty-Fifth Dynasty--Nubians, successors of
      Piankhy; Assyrian Invasion
         Amenirdis II

Twenty-Sixth Dynasty of Sais.
      Assyrian oversight; Greek mercantile
         colonies
      Psammetichus I and Mehytemwaskhet
      Nitocris  656 B.C.
         Ankhnesneferibre

Twenty Seventh Dynasty -- First Persian
      Conquest             525-404

Native Dynasties:
      Twenty-Eighth--Saite Dynasty
      Twenty-Ninth  and Thirtieth

Thirty-First Dynasty -- Second Persian Conquest

      Conquest by Alexander the Great 332 B.C.

## Ptolemaic Period -- ruling from Alexandria
on the Mediterranean -- 332-30 B.C.
      Deified queens.
      Cleopatra VII ended dynasty as last ruler
         of an independent Egypt

## Roman Period 30 B.C.-395 A.D.

The Lady Nofret from an early Fourth
Dynasty tomb at Meidum.
Courtesy of the Egyptian Museum, Cairo

# *Bibliography*

## Goddesses and Queens:

**Adams**, B. 1992. "Curator's Choice: A Predynastic Female Figurine," *KMT: a Modern Journal of ancient Egypt.* March: 12-13.

_____.1988. *Predynastic Egypt.* Aylesbury, Bucks: Princes Risborough.

**Allen**, J. P. 1994. "Nefertiti and Smenkh-ka-re," *Göttinger Miszellen* 141: 7-13.

**Arnold,** D. & A. Oppenheim. 1995. "Reexcavating the Senwosret III Pyramid Complex at Dahshur," *KMT: A Modern Journal of Ancient Egypt.* vol. 6, no. 2. 44-56.

**Baumgartel**, E. J. 1955. *The Culture of Prehistoric Egypt.* London: Oxford University Press.

_____. 1970. "Predynastic Egypt," chapter IX in *The Cambridge Ancient History,* Third Edition, Vol. 1, Part 1.

**Bietak**, M. 1995. "Avaris and the Aegean in the Early 18th dynasty: New Finds from Tell el-Dab'a," *Seventh International Congress of Egyptologists, Abstracts.* Cambridge: Oxbow Press, 21.

**Blankenberg-van Delden**, C. 1982. "A Genealogical Reconstruction of the Kings and Queens of the Late 17th and early 18th Dynasties," *Göttinger Miszellen* 54: 31-45.

**Bleeker**, C. 1967. "The Position of the Queen in ancient Egypt," *The Sacral Kingship.* Leiden: 1967

_____. 1973. *Hathor and Thoth.* Leiden: Brill.

**Breasted**, J. H. 1906. *Ancient Records of Egypt, III.* New York: Russell & Russell, re-issue 1962.

**Bryan**, B. M. 1984. "Evidence of Female Literacy from Theban Tombs of the New Kingdom," *Bulletin of the Egyptological Seminar,* 6: 17-32.

_____. 1991. *The Reign of Thutmose IV.* Baltimore & London: The Johns Hopkins University Press.

**de Buck**, A. 1937. "The Judicial Papyrus of Turin," *Journal of Egyptian Archaeology* 23: 153-157.

**Callender**, V. G. 1992. "Female Officials in Ancient Egypt and Egyptian Historians," *Stereotypes of Women in Power: Historical Perspectives and Revisionist Views.* Ed. B. Garlick, S. Dixon and P. Allen. New York: Greenwood Press.

**Clagett**, M. 1989. *Ancient Egyptian Science: A Source Book,* I Philadelphia: American Philosophical Society.

**Cron**, R. L. & G. B. Johnson. 1995. "De Morgan at Dahshur," Part One. *KMT: A Modern Journal of ancient Egypt,* vol. 6, no. 2.34-43.

**Desroches-Noblecourt**, C. and C. Kuentz, 1968. *Le Petit Temple d'Abou Simbel* Caire: Ministere de la Culture, Centre de documentation et d'étude sur l'ancienne Égypte, 2 vols.

**Dodson**, A. 1973. The Takhats and some other royal Ladies of the Ramesside Period," *Journal of Egyptian Archaeology* 59 : 224-29.

**Dorman**, P. F. 1988. *The Monuments of Senenmut: Problems in Historical Methodology.* London & New York: Kegan Paul International.

**Dunham**, D. and **Simpson**, Wm. K. 1974. *The Mastaba of Queen Mersyankh III G 7530-7540.* Boston: Museum of Fine Arts.

**Edwards**, I.E.S. 1971. "The Early Dynastic Period in Egypt," *The Cambridge Ancient History*, I, Part 2, Chapter XI, 3rd ed. Cambridge: University Press.

**Epigraphic Survey**, University of Chicago. 1980. *The Tomb of Kheruef, Theban Tomb 192*. Oriental Institute Publication 102, Chicago: University of Chicago Press.

**Fischer**, H. G. 1982. "Priesterin," in *Lexikon der Ägyptologie* IV, Wiesbaden: Harrasowitz, cols. 1100-1105.

**Gardiner**, A. H. 1946. "Davies's copy of the great Speos Artemidos Inscription," *Journal of Egyptian Archaeology* 32: 43-56 + double plate.

**Gitton**, M. 1975. *L'Épouse du Dieu Ahmes Nefertary*. Paris: Les Belles Lettres.

_____. 1984. *Les Divines Épouses de la 18ie dynastie*. Paris: Les Belles Lettres.

**Goedicke**, H. 1954. "An Approximate Date for the Harem Investigation under Pepy I," *Journal of the American Oriental Society* 74, 88-89.

_____. 1973. "Was Magic Used in the Harem Conspiracy against Ramesses III?" *Journal of Egyptian Archaeology* 49, 71-92.

**Goetze**, A. 1955. "Suppiluliumas and the Egyptian Queen" in *Ancient Near Eastern Texts*, ed. J. B. Pritchard, 2nd ed. Princeton University Press, p. 319.

**Gohary**, J. 1979. "Nefertiti at Karnak," in J. Ruffle et al ed. *Glimpses of ancient Egypt*. Warminster: Aris & Phillips. 30-31.

**Grimal**, N. 1992. *A History of Ancient Egypt*. Oxford: Blackwell.

**Habachi**, L. 1957. Two Graffiti at Sehel from the Reign of Queen Hatshepsut. *Journal of Near Eastern Studies:* 16, 88-104.

_____. 1969. *"La reine Touy, femme de Sethi I et ses proches parents inconnue,"* Revue d'Égyptologie 21: 27-47.

_____. 1977. *The Obelisks of Egypt: skyscrapers of the past*. New York: Scribners.

**Hankey**, V. "Egypt, the Aegean and the Levant," *Egyptian Archaeology: the Bulletin of The Egypt Exploration Society*, No. 3, 1993, 27-29.

**Harris**, J. R. 1973a. "Nefertiti Rediviva," *Acta Orientalia* 35: 5-13.

_____. 1973b. "Neferneferuaten," *Gottinger Miszellen* 4: 15-17.

**Hayes**, Wm. C. 1953. *Scepter of Egypt, I*, New York: Metropolitan Museum of Art.

**Helck**, W. 1972-80. 1980. *Lexikon der Ägyptologie* ed. with E. Otto & W. Westendorf. Wiesbaden: Harrassowitz.

**Heyob**, S. K. 1975. *The Cult of Isis among women in the Graeco- Roman World*. Leiden: Brill.

**Hollis**, S. 1994/5. "Five Egyptian goddesses in the Third Millennium B.C.," in *KMT: A Modern Journal of ancient Egypt*.

**Killen**, G. 1980. *Ancient Egyptian Furniture*. 2 vols. Warminster: Aris & Phillips.

**Kitchen**, K. A. 1982. *Pharaoh Triumphant: the life and times of Ramses II, King of Egypt*. Warminster: Aris & Phillips.

_____. 1962. *Suppiluliumas and the Amarna Pharaohs: A Study in Relative Chronology*. Liverpool: Liverpool University Press.

_____. 1973. *The Third Intermediate Period in Egypt (1100-650 B.C.)* Warminster: Aris & Phillips.

**Kuchman**, L. 1977-78. "The Titles of Queenship," Part 1 & 2 , *Society for the Study of Egyptian Archaeology Newsletter* 7/3: 9/1: 21-25.

**Kuchman-Sabbahy**, L. 1981. "The Titulary of Queens Nbt and Hnwt," *Göttinger Miszellen* 52: 37-42.

**Lacau**, P. and Chevrier, H. 1977 & 1979. *Une chapelle d'Hatchepsout a Karnak*, 2 vols. Cairo: l'Institut français d'archéologie orientale.

**Leacock**, E. B. 1981. *Myths of Male Dominance*. New York: Monthly Review Press.

**Lesko**, B. S. 1967. "The Senmut Problem," *Journal of the American Research Center in Egypt* 6:113-118.

**Lesko**, L. H. 1966. "A Little More Evidence for the end of the Nineteenth Dynasty," *Journal of the American Research Center in Egypt* 5: 29-32.

_____. 1991. "Ancient Egyptian Cosmogonies and Cosmology," in B. E. Shafer ed. *Religion in Ancient Egypt*. Ithaca: Cornell University Press.

**Lichtheim**, M. 1973. *Ancient Egyptian Literature* I: The Old and Middle Kingdoms. Berkeley: University of California Press.

**Lorton**, D. 1974. Review of Reiser, *Der Konigliche Harim* in *Journal of the American Research Center in Egypt* 11: 98-101.

**Malek**, J. 1986 *In the Shadow of the Pyramids*. Norman: University of Oklahoma Press.

**Martin**, G. 1979. "Queen Mutnodjmet at Memphis and El-Amarna," *L'égyptologie en 1979* II, 275-78.

**Menu**, B. 1977. "La stele d'Ahmes-Nefertary dans son contexte historique et juridique," *Bulletin de l'Institut Français d'Archéologie Orientale*, 77: 89-100.

**Montet**, P. 1957. "Reines et pyramides," *Kemi* 14 : 92-101.

**Moran**, Wm. L. ed. 1992. *The Amarna Letters*. Baltimore: Johns Hopkins University Press.

**Morkot**, R. 1986. "Violent Images of Queenship and the Royal cult," *Wepwawet* 2: 1-9.

**Naville**, E. 1907-13. *The XIth dynasty Temple at Deir el-Bahari*, 3 vols. London: Egypt Exploration Fund.

_____. 1894-1908. *The Temple of Deir el Bahari*. 7 vols. London: Egypt Exploration Fund.

**Newberry**, P. E. 1943. "Queen Nitocris of the Sixth Dynasty," *Journal of Egyptian Archaeology* 29: 51-54.

**Nims**, C. 1966. "The Date of the Dishonoring of Hatshepsut," *Zeitschrift für aegyptische Sprache* 93: 97-100.

**Nord**, D. 1970. review of Reiser, *Der königliche Harim* in *Journal of Near Eastern Studies*, 34: 142-145.

____. 1970a "Ḫkrt-nswt= 'King's Concubine'?" *Serapis* 2 , 1-16.

____. 1981. "The Term ḫnr 'harem' or 'musical performers'" in Wm. K. Simpson & W. V. Davies eds. *Studies in ancient Egypt, the Aegean, and the Sudan*. Boston: Museum of Fine Arts, 137-145.

**Nur el-Din**, M. A. 1980. "Some Remarks on the Title 'mwt-nsw'," *Orientalia Lovaniensia Periodica* 11 : 91-98.

**Petrie**, W. M. F. et al 1912. *The Labyrinth, Gerzeh, and Mazghuneh*. Egyptian Research Account 21. London: School of Archaeology in Egypt.

**Ratie**, A. 1979. *La reine Hatchepsout*. Leiden: Brill.

**Redford**, D. B. 1967. *History and Chronology of the Eighteenth Dynasty*, Toronto: University of Toronto Press.

**Reiser**, E. 1972. *Die Königliche harim im alten Ägypten und seine verwaltung*. Vienna: Verlag Notring.

**Robins**, G. 1983. "The God's Wife of Amon in the 18th dynasty in Egypt," in A. Cameron and Kuhrt, A. *Images of Women in Antiquity*. Detroit: 65-78.

**Saleh**, M. & H. Sourouzian. 1987. The Egyptian Museum Cairo: Official Catalogue. Mainz: Von Zabern.

**Samson**, J. 1979. "Akhenaten's Successor," *Göttinger Miszellen* 32: 53-58.

_____. 1985. *Nefertiti and Cleopatra*. London: Rubicon

**Staehelin**, E. 1982. "Menit," in *Lexikon der Ägyptologie* IV: cols. 246-248.

**Te Velde**, H. 1982. "Mut," in *Lexikon der Ägyptologie* IV: cols. 246-248.

_____. 1982. "The Cat as Sacred Animal of the goddess Mut," *Studies in Egyptian Religion dedicated to Professor Jan Zandee*. Leiden: Brill: 127-137.

**Troy**, L. 1986. *Patterns of Queenship in ancient Egyptian Myth and History. Acta Universitatis Upsaliensis Boreas.* Uppsala Studies in Ancient Mediterranean and Near Eastern Civilizations 14.

**Ucko**, P. 1968. *Anthropomorphic Figurines of Pre-dynastic Egypt and Neolithic Crete with Comparative Material for the Prehistoric Near East and Mainland Greece*. London: Andrew Szmidla.

**Van Siclen**, C.C. 1992. "Egyptian Antiquties in South Texas, part 2." *Varia Aegyptiaca* 8.

_____. 1995. "Queen Meryetre-Hatshepsut and the Edifice of Amenhotep II at Karnak," Seventh International Association of Egyptologists Congress *Abstracts*, Cambridge: Oxbow Books.

**Verner**, M. 1980. "Die Königsmutter Chentkaus von Abusir und einige Bemerkungen zur Geschichte der 5. Dynastie," *Studien zur altägyptischen Kultur* 8: 243-268.

**Wente**, E. 1969. "Hathor at the Jubilee," in G. Kadesh ed. *Studies in Honor of John A. Wilson*. Studies in Ancient Oriental Civilizations, 35 Chicago: The Oriental Institute.

_____. 1990. *Letters from Ancient Egypt*. Society of Biblical Literature. Writings from the Ancient World, I, Atlanta: Scholars Press.

**Werbrouck**, M. 1948. *Le Temple d'Hatshepsout a Deir el Bahari*, Brussels: Fondation égyptologique Reine Elisabeth.

**Winlock**, H. 1942. *Excavations at Deir el Bahri 1911-1931*. New York: The Macmillan Company.

**Wysocki**, Z. 1986. "The Temple of Queen Hatshepsut at Deir el Bahari: its original form." *Mitteilungen des Deutschen Archäologischen Instituts*, Abteilung Kairo 42: 213-228.

**Zivie**, C. M. 1982. "Nitokris," in W. Helck and E. Otto eds. *Lexikon der Ägyptologie* cols. 513-14.

## Non-royal Women

**Allam**, S. 1971. "Familie," in W. Helck and E. Otto eds. *Lexikon der Ägyptologie* cols. 104-09.

_____. 1985. *Everyday Life in Ancient Egypt.* Guizeh: Foreign Cultural Information Dept.

_____. 1989. "Women as Owners of Immovables in Pharaonic Egypt," in B. S. Lesko ed. *Women's Earliest Records from ancient Egypt and Western Asia.* Atlanta: Scholar's Press.

_____. 1990. "Women as Holders of Rights in ancient Egypt (during the Late Period," *Journal of the Economic and Social History of the Orient,* Vol. XXXII, 1-32.

**Baer**, K. 1963. "An Eleventh Dynasty Farmer's Letters to His Family," *Journal of the American Oriental Society* 83 (1963): 1-19.

**Bierbrier**, M. 1973. "Herere, wife of the High Priest Piankhi," *Journal of Near Eastern Studies* 32 : 311.

_____. 1975. *The Late New Kingdom in Egypt,* Warminster: Aris & Phillips.

_____. 1980. "Terms of Relationship at Deir el Medina," *Journal of Egyptian Archaeology* 66: 100-107.

_____. 1982. *The Tomb-builders of the Pharaohs.* London: British Museum.

**Blackman**, A.M. 1921. "On the Position of Women in the ancient Egyptian Hierarchy," *Journal of Egyptian Archaeology* 7 : 8-30.

**Borghouts**, J. F. 1982. "Divine Intervention in ancient Egypt and its Manifestation (b3w)," R. J. Demaree & J. Janssen eds. *Gleanings from Deir el Medina.* Leiden: Brill: 1-70.

_____. 1981. "Montu and Matrimonial Squabbles," *Revue d'Egyptologie* 33 : 11-22.

_____. 1994. "Magical Practices among the Villagers," in L. H. Lesko ed. *Pharaoh's Workers: the villagers of Deir el Medina.* Ithaca: Cornell University Press.

**Breasted**, J. H. Jr. 1948. *Egyptian Servant Statues.* New York: 1948.

**Bryan**, B. M. 1984a. "Non-Royal Women's titles in the 18th Egyptian Dynasty," *American Research Center in Egypt Newsletter,* 113-16.

_____. 1984b. "Evidence of Female Literacy from Theban Tombs of the New Kingdom," *BES* 6, 17-32.

**Caminos**, R. 1964. "The Nitocris Adoption Stela," *Journal of Egyptian Archaeology* 4, 107-118.

**Černý**, J. 1945. "The Will of Naunakhte and the Related Documents," *Journal of Egyptian Archaeology* 31: 29-53.

_____. 1954. "Consanguineous Marriage in Pharaonic Egypt," *Journal of Egyptian Archaeology* 40: 23-29.

_____. 1957. "A Note on the ancient Egyptian Family," *Studi in onore di A. Calderini e R. Paraibeni* II: 51-55.

_____. 1973. *A Community of Workmen at Thebes in the Ramesside Period.* Bibliotheque d'Etude 50. Cairo: Institut Fançais d'Archéologie Orientale.

**Černý**, J. and T. E. **Peet** 1927. "A Marriage Settlement of the Twentieth Dynasty," *Journal of Egyptian Archaeology* 13: 30-39.

**Davies**, N. de G. 1920. *The tomb of Antefoker, Vizier of Sesostris I, and his wife, Senet.* London: Egypt Exploration Fund.

_____ and A. H. **Gardiner**. 1915. *The Tomb of Amenemhet (No 82).* London: Egypt Exploration Fund.

**Desroches-Noblecourt**, C. 1953. "Concubines du Mort et meres de familie au Moyen Empire, *Bulletin de l'Institut Francais d'Archéologie Orientale,* 53 : 7-47.

**Edgerton**, W. F. 1951. "The Strikes in Ramses III's Twenty-ninth Year," *Journal of Near Eastern Studies,* 10: 137-145.

**El-Amir**, M. 1962. "Monogamy, Polygamy, Endogamy, and Consanguinity in ancient Egyptian Marriage," *Bulletin de l'Institut français d'Archéologie Orientale du Caire* 62 : 103-107.

**Eyre**, C. J. 1984. "Crime and Adultery in Ancient Egypt." *Journal of Egyptian Archaeology* 70 : 92-105.

_____. 1992. "The Adoption Papyrus in Social Context," Journal of Egyptian Archaeology 78: 207-221.

**Fischer**, H. W. 1956. "A Daughter of the Overlords of Upper Egypt in the First Intermediate Period," *Journal of the American Oriental Society* 76 : 99-110.

_____. 1976. *Varia: Egyptian Studies* I. New York.

_____. 1982. "Priesterin," in W. Helck and E. Otto eds. *Lexikon der Ägyptologie.* Wiesbaden, IV : cols. 1100-1105.

_____. 1989. "Women in the Old Kingdom and the Heracleopolitan Period," in B. S. Lesko ed. *Women's Earliest Records from Ancient Egypt and Western Asia.* Atlanta: Scholars Press: 5-24.

**Fox**, M. V. 1985. *The Song of Songs and Ancient Egyptian Love Songs.* Madison: University of Wisconsin Press.

**Friedman**, F. 1994. "Aspects of Domestic Life and Religion," in L. H. Lesko ed., *Pharaoh's Workers: The Villagers of Deir el Medina.* Ithaca: Cornell University Press: 95-117.

**Gaballa**, G. A. 1977. *The Memphite Tomb-chapel of Mose.* Warminster: Aris and Phillips.

**Galvin**, M. 1981. *The Priestesses of Hathor in the Old Kingdom and 1st Intermediate Period.* (Brandeis University Dissertation) Ann Arbor: University Microfilm.

_____. 1984. "The Hereditary Status of the Titles of the Cult of Hathor," *Journal of Egyptian Archaeology* 70: 42-49.

_____. 1989. "Addendum," in B. Lesko ed. *Women's Earliest Records from ancient Egypt and Western Asia.* Atlanta: Scholars Press.

**Gardiner**, A. H. 1906. "Four Papyri of the18th dynasty from Kahun," *Zeitschrift für Aegyptische Sprache* 43: 27-54.

_____. 1935. "A Lawsuit arising from the Purchase of Two Slaves," *Journal of Egyptian Archaeology* 21: 140-146.

_____. 1940. "Adoption Extraordinary," *Journal of Egyptian Archaeology* 26: 23-29.

**Gillam**, R. 1995. "Priestesses of Hathor: Their Function, Decline and Disappearance," *Journal of the American Research Center in Egypt* 32: 211-237.

**Gitton**, M. 1976. "Le rôle des femmes dans le clergé d'Amon a la 18e dynastie," *Bulletin de Societe français d'Égyptologie,* 75.

_____. 1977. "Gottesgemählin," *Lexikon der Ägyptologie,* 2, cols.: 792-812.

**Goedicke**, H. 1973. "Was Magic Used in the Harem conspiracy against Ramesses III?" *Journal of Egyptian Archaeology* 49, 71-92.

**Gunn**, B. 1916. "The Religion of the Poor," *Journal of Egyptian Archaeology* 3: 81-94.

_____, and I.E.S. Edwards, 1955. "The Decree of Amonrasonther for Neskhons," *Journal of Egyptian Archaeology* 41: 83-105.

**Hall**, R. 1986. *Egyptian Textiles.* Aylesbury: Princes Risborough.

**Harari**, I. 1983. "La capacité juridique de la femme au Nouvel Empire," *Revue Internationale des Droits de l'Antiquité,* 3rd series, 30: 41-54.

**Harer**, W. B. and Z. el-Dawakhly, 1989. "Peseshet: the first Female Physician?," *Obstetrics & Gynecology* 74: 960-61.

**Hawass**, Z. 1992. "Recent Discoveries at Giza Plateau." *Atti VI.* Torino: Congresso Internazionale Egittologia, I, 241-2.

**Hayes**, Wm.C. 1955. *A Papyrus of the Late Middle Kingdom in the Brooklyn Museum.* Brooklyn: The Brooklyn Museum.

**Hickman**, H. 1954. "La menat," *Kemi,* 13: 99-102.

**Hohenwart-Gerlachstein**, A. 1955. "The Legal Position of Women in Ancient Egypt," *Wiener Völkerkundliche Mitteilungen,* 3, Jahrgang Nr. 1: 90 ff.

**James**, T.G.H. 1962. *The Hekanakhte Papers and other Early Middle Kingdom Documents,* New York: Metropolitan Museum of Art.

**Janssen**, J. J. 1975. *Commodity Prices from the Ramesside Period.* Leiden: Brill.

_____. 1988. "Marriage Problems and Public Reactions (P.BM 10416)," in J. Baines et al eds. *Pyramid Studies and other Essays presented to I.E.S. Edwards,* London: Egypt Exploration Society, 134-137.

_____. 1992. "Literacy and Letters at Deir el-Medina," in R. J. Demaree and A. Egberts, ed. *Village Voices: Proceedings of the symposium "Texts from Deir el-Medina and their Interpretation"* Leiden, May 31-June 1, 1991. Leiden: Centre of Non-Western Studies, Leiden University, 81-94.

**Janssen**, J. J. and P. W. Pestman. 1968. "Burial and Inheritance in the Community of the Necropolis Workmen at Thebes," *Journal of the Economic and Social History of the Orient* 11: 137-170.

**Janssen**, R. M. and J. J. 1990. *Growing Up in ancient Egypt,* London: Rubicon.

**Johnson**, J. H. 1994. "'Annuity contracts' and Marriage," in D. Silverman ed. *For His Ka: Essays offered in Memory of Klaus Baer.* Studies in Ancient Oriental Civilization, No. 55. Chicago: University of Chicago Press, 113-132.

_____. 1996. "The Legal Status of Women in ancient Egypt," *Mistress of House, Mistress of Heaven,* exhibition catalogue of Cincinnati Art Museum. New York: Hudson Hills Press.

**Kanawati**, N. 1976. "Polygamy in the Old Kingdom," in *Studien zur Aegyptische Sprache und Altertumskunde* 4: 149-60.

**Kemp**, B. 1987. "The Amarna Workmen's Village in Retrospect," *Journal of Egyptian Archaeology* 73: 21-50.

_____. 1979. "Wall Paintings from the workmen's Village at el-Amarna," *Journal of Egyptian Archaeology* 65: 47-52.

_____. 1989. *Ancient Egypt: Anatomy of a Civilization.* London: Routledge.

**Kitchen**, K. A. 1978. *Ramesside Inscriptions.* III, Oxford: Blackwell.

**Kruchten**, J.-M. 1981. *Le Décret d'Horemheb.* Bruxelles: Éditions de l'Université de Bruxelles.

**Lesko**, B. S. 1986. "True Art in Ancient Egypt," in L. H. Lesko, ed. *Egyptological Studies in Honor of Richard A. Parker.* Hanover: University Press of New England, 85-97.

_____. 1987. "Women of Egypt and the Ancient Near East," in R. Bridenthal, C. Koonz, S. Stuard ed. *Becoming Visible: Women in European History.* 2nd ed. Boston: Houghton Mifflin Company.

_____. 1991. "Women's Monumental Mark on ancient Egypt." *Biblical Archaeologist,* 54/1: 4-15.

_____. 1994. "Rank, Roles, and Rights," in L. H. Lesko ed. *Pharaoh's Workers: The Villagers of Deir el Medina,* Ithaca: Cornell University Press..

_____. 1996. "The Rhetoric of Women in Ancient Egypt," in M.M. Wertheimer ed. *Essays on the Rhetorical Activities of Historical Women.* Columbia S.C.: University of South Carolina Press.

**Lesko**, L.H. 1966. "A Little More Evidence for the End of the Nineteenth Dynasty," *Journal of the American Research Center in Egypt,* 5, 29-32.

_____. 1986. "Three Late Egyptian Stories Reconsidered." in idem, ed. *Egyptological Studies in Honor of Richard A. Parker.* Hanover: University Press of New England: 98-103.

_____. 1994b. "Some Remarks on the Books of the Dead Composed for the High Priests Pinedjem I and II," in D. Silverman ed. *For his Ka: Essays Offered in Memory of Klaus Baer.* Chicago: The Oriental Institute: 179-186.

**Lichtheim**, M. 1973 & 1976. *Ancient Egyptian Literature Vol. 1 & II: The Old and Middle Kingdoms; The New Kingdom.* Berkeley: University of California Press.

_____. 1988. *Ancient Egyptian Autobiographies chiefly of the Middle Kingdom: a study and anthology.* Freiburg, Schweiz: Universitätsverlag.

**Lorton**, D. 1995. "Legal and social Institutions of Pharaonic Egypt" in J. Sasson ed. *Civilizations of the Ancient Near East.* New York: Scribners: 345-362.

**Mace**, A. C. & H. E. Winlock, 1916, rpt. 1973. *The Tomb of Senebtisi at Lisht.* New York: Metropolitan Museum of Art. Reprint Arno Press.

**Malaise**, M. 1977. "La Position de la Femme sur les Stéles du Moyen Empire," *Studien zur altaegyptischen Kultur,* 5: 183-193.

**Manniche**, L. 1987. *Sexual Life in ancient Egypt.* London.

_____.1991. *Music and Musicians in ancient Egypt.* London.

**McDowell**, A.G. 1990. *Jurisdiction in the Workmen's Community of Deir el-Medina.* Leiden: Brill.

_____. 1994. "Contact with the Outside World," in L. H. Lesko ed. *Pharaoh's Workers.* Ithaca: Cornell University Press: 41-59.

**Menu**, B. 1982. *Recherches sur l'histoire juridique, économique et sociale de l'ancienne Égypte.* Versailles: B. Menu.

_____. 1989. "Women and Business Life in the First Millennium B.C.," in B. S. Lesko ed. *Women's Earliest Records,* Atlanta: Scholars Press: 193-205.

**Middleton**, R. 1962. "Brother-sister and Father-daughter marriage in Ancient Egypt," *American Sociological Review,* 27: 603-611.

**Millard**, A. 1976. *The Position of Women in Society and in the family in ancient Egypt, with special reference to the Middle Kingdom.* (Unpublished dissertation), University College London. 3 vols.

**Morkot**, R. 1986. "Violent Images of Queenship," *Wepwawet* 2: 1-9.

**Naguib**, S. 1988. *La Clergé Féminin d'Amon Thébain a la 21ᵉ Dynastie.* Oslo: Etnografisk Museum.

**Newberry**, P. E. 1893-1900. *Beni Hasan* 4 vols. London: Egypt Exploration Fund.

**Nims**, C. 1958. "Some Notes on the Family of Mereruka," *Journal of the American Oriental Society,* 58: 638-647.

**Niwinski**, A. 1988. "The Wives of Pinudjem II," *Journal of Egyptian Archaeology,* 74: 226-30.

_____. 1989. "Some Remarks on Rank and Titles of Women in the Twenty-first Dynasty Theban State of Amun." *Discussions in Egyptology*, 14: 81-89.

**Nord**, D. 1981. "The term *ḫnr* 'harem' or 'musical performers' in Wm. K, Simpson & W. V. Davies eds. *Studies in ancient Egypt, the Aegean and the Sudan*. Boston: Museum of Fine Arts: 137-145.

**Ogdon**, J. R. 1986. "An Exceptional Family of Priests of the Early Fifth Dynasty at Giza," *Göttinger Miszellen*, 90: 61-65.

**Omlin**, J. 1973. *Der Papyrus 55001 und seine satirische-erotischen Zeichnungen und Inschriften*, Turin: Editioni d Arte Fratelli Pozzo.

**Peet**, T. E. 1930. *The Great Tomb Robberies of the Twentieth Egyptian Dynasty*. 2 vols. Oxford: Clarendon Press.

**Pestman**, P. W. 1961. *Marriage and Matrimonial Property in Ancient Egypt*. (Papyrologica Lugduno-Batava, 9), Leiden: Brill.

**Pfluger**, K. 1947. "The Private Funerary Stelae of the Middle Kingdom and their Importance for the Study of Ancient Egyptian History," *Journal of the American Oriental Society*, 67: 127-135.

**Pinch**, G. 1983. "Childbirth and Female Figurines at Deir el-Medina and el-Amarna." *Orientalia*, 52: 405-414.

_____. 1989. *Votive Offerings to Hathor*. Warminster: Aris and Phillips.

_____. 1995. "Private Life in Ancient Egypt," in J. Sasson ed. *Near Eastern Civilizations*: 363-381.

**Pirenne**, J. 1959. "La statut de la Femme dans l'ancienne Égypte," *Recueils de la Société Jean Bodin* XI: 63-77.

**Simpson**, Wm. K. 1974. "Polygamy in Egypt in the Middle Kingdom," *Journal of Egyptian Archaeology* 60: 100-105.

**Smither**, P. 1948. "The Report Concerning the Slave Girl Senbet," *Journal of Egyptian Archaeology*, 34: 31-34.

**Sweeney**, D. 1993. "Women's Correspondence from Deir el-Medineh," *Sesto Congresso Internazionale di Egittologia, Atti:* 523-529.

**Theodorides**, A. 1976. "Le Droit matrimonial dans l'Égypte pharaonique," *Revue International de Droit Ancienne*, 3e Serie, 23: 15-55.

_____. 1977. "Frau," in W. Helck and E. Otto eds. *Lexikon der Ägyptologie*, II. 280-295.

**Troy**, L. 1984. "Good and Bad Women: Maxim 18/284-288 of the Instructions of Ptahhotep." *Göttinger Miszellen* 80: 77-81.

**Vercoutter**, J. 1965. "La Femme en Egypte Ancienne," in *Histoire Mondiale de la Femme* ed. P. Grimal, Paris: Nouvelle Libraire de France: 43-69.

**Ward**, Wm. A. 1982. *Index of Egyptian Administrative and Religious Titles of the Middle Kingdom*, Beirut; 1982.

_____ 1986. *Essays on feminine Titles of the Middle Kingdom and Related Subjects*. Beirut: American University Press.

_____ 1989. "Non-royal Women and their Occupations in the Middle Kingdom," in B. S. Lesko (ed.) *Women's Earliest Records from Ancient Egypt and Western Asia*. Atlanta: Scholars Press: 33-43.

**Wenig**, S. 1969. *The Woman in Egyptian Art*. translated by B. Fischer. Leipzig: Edition Leipzig.

**Wente**, E. F. 1990. *Letters from Ancient Egypt*. Atlanta: Scholars Press.

**Whale**, S. 1989. *The Family in the Eighteenth Dynasty of Egypt: A Study of the Representation of the Family in Private Tombs*. Sydney: Australian Centre for Egyptology.

**White**, J. B. 1978. *A Study of the Language of Love in the Song of Songs and ancient Egyptian Poetry*. Missoula: Scholars Press.

**Wildung**, D. 1984. "Nouveaux aspects de la femme en Égypte pharaonique." *Bulletin de societe Français égyptienne*, 102: 9-26.

**Willems**, H. O. 1983. "A Description of Egyptian Kinship Terminology of the Middle Kingdom," *Bijdragen, tot de Taal, Land en Volenkunde*, 139: 152-168.

## General Works, Histories and Collections:

**Aldred**, C. 1971. *Jewels of the Pharaohs*, London: Thames and Hudson.

**Bierbrier**, M. 1975. *The Late New Kingdom in Egypt*, Warminster: Aris & Phillips.

**Bietak**, M. 1992. "Minoan Wall Paintings unearthed at Ancient Avaris." *Egyptian Archaeology, Bulletin of the Egypt Exploration Society*, No. 2.

**Bourreau**, J. 1988. *Pharaohs and Mortals*, Cambridge: Cambridge University Press.

**Breasted**, J. H. 1906. *Ancient Records of Egypt*. re-issue 1962, 5 vols. New York: Russell & Russell.

**Brovarski**, E. et al 1982. *Egypt's Golden Age: the art of living in the New Kingdom. Catalogue of the Exhibition.* Boston: Museum of Fine Arts .

**Demareé**, R. J. & A. Egberts. 1992. *Village Voices.* Leiden: Centre of Non-Western Studies, Leiden University.

**Desroches-Noblecourt**, C. 1993. *La femme au temps des Pharaons.* Paris: Editions Stock.

**Edwards**, I.E.S., Gadd, C.J. and Hammond, N.G. 1971. *Cambridge Ancient History*, I:2 The Early History of the Middle East. 3rd ed. Cambridge.

————. 1973. *Cambridge Ancient History*, II. 1-2. History of the Middle East and the Aegean Region c. 1800-1380 and c. 1380-1000. 3rd ed. Cambridge.

**Fischer**, H. G. 1985. *Egyptian Titles of the Middle Kingdom*, (3 parts), New York:

**Grimal**, N. 1992. *A History of Ancient Egypt*, Translated by I. Shaw. Oxford: Blackwell.

**James**, T.G.H. 1984. *Pharaoh's People: Scenes from Life in Imperial Egypt*, Chicago: University of Chicago Press.

**Kemp**, B. 1991. *Ancient Egypt: Anatomy of a Civilization*, London and New York: Routledge.

**Killen**, G. A. 1980. *Ancient Egyptian Furniture.* Warminster: Aris & Phillips, Vol. I.

**Kitchen**, K. A. 1973. *The Third Intermediate Period in Egypt*, Warminster: Aris & Phillips.

**Kozloff**, A. and B. M. Bryan. 1992. *Egypt's Dazzling Sun: Amenhotep III and his world*, Cleveland: Museum of Art.

**Lesko**, B. S. 1989. ed. *Women's Earliest Records from Ancient Egypt and Western Asia*, Atlanta: Scholars Press.

**Lesko**, L. H. 1994. ed. *Pharaoh's Workers: The Villagers of Deir el Medina*, Ithaca: Cornell University Press.

**Lichtheim**, M. 1973-1980. *Ancient Egyptian Literature*, 3 vols. Berkeley: University of California Press.

**Malek**, J. 1986. *In the Shadow of the Pyramids: Egypt during the Old Kingdom*, Norman: Oklahoma Press.

**Nur el Din**, A. H. 1995. *The Role of Women in the Ancient Egyptian Society*, Cairo: S.C.A. Press.

**Robins**, G. 1993. *Women in Ancient Egypt*, Cambridge: Harvard University Press.

**Sasson**, J. M. ed. 1995. *Civilizations of the Ancient Near East*, New York: Charles Scribners, 4 volumes.

**Shafer**, B. E. 1991. ed. *Religion in Ancient Egypt: Gods, Myths, and Personal Practice*, Ithaca: Cornell University Press.

**Tyldesley**, 1994. *Daughters of Isis: Women of ancient Egypt*, London: Viking Press.

**Watterson**, B. 1991. *Women in Ancient Egypt*, New York: St. Martin's Press.